W9-BVM-228

On Good Land

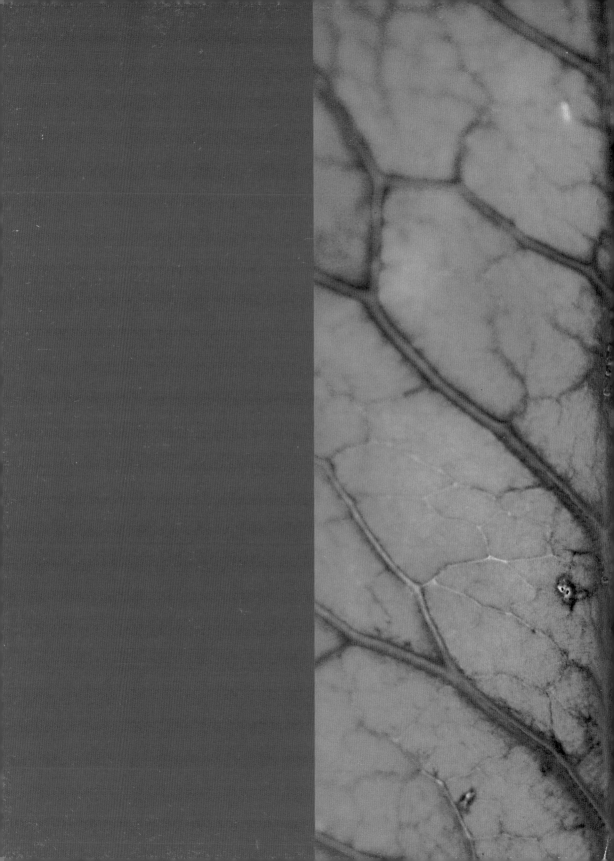

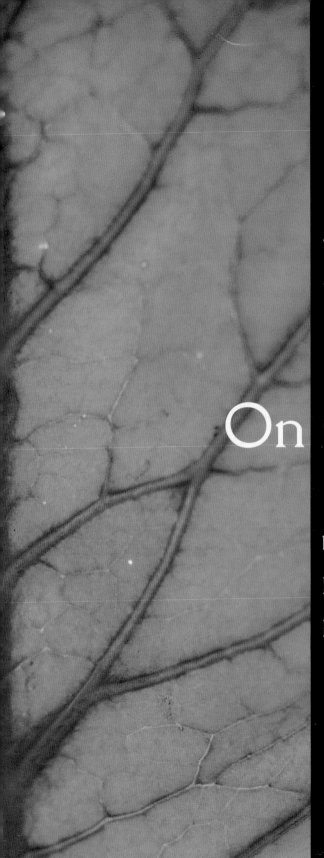

The Autobiography
of an Urban Farm

On Good Land

by Michael Ableman

Foreword by Alice Waters

Edited by Cynthia Wisehart

CHRONICLE BOOKS
SAN FRANCISCO

In Memory of Roger Chapman and John Collier

Library of Congress Cataloging-in-Publication Data :

Ableman, Michael
    On good land: the autobiography of an urban farm / by Michael
  Ableman : foreword by Alice Waters.
      144 p.   16.5 x 22.9 cm.
      ISBN 0-8118-1921-3
      1. Organic farming—California—Santa Barbara. 2. Fairview
  Gardens (Santa Barbara, Calif.)—History. 3. Ableman, Michael.
      4. Farmers—California—Biography. I. Title.
      S605.5.A25   1998
      635'.092—dc21
      [B]   97-30801
                                                       CIP

Printed in Hong Kong.

Designed by Laura Lovett

Distributed in Canada by Raincoast Books
8680 Cambie Street
Vancouver, B.C. V6P 6M9

10 9 8 7 6 5 4 3 2 1

Chronicle Books
85 Second Street
San Francisco, CA 94105

Web Site: www.chronbooks.com

Contents

Foreword

For years now, my family and I have been making an annual wintertime visit to Michael Ableman and his family at Fairview Gardens. It's become a holiday tradition I look forward to all year: harvesting and preparing food and sharing long, happy meals around the farmhouse table. When it's my turn to cook, I have the rare pleasure of planning the menu while wandering through fields and orchards, collecting ingredients as I go from among hundreds of varieties of fruits and vegetables.

I've gotten to know Michael better and better over the years and we've become good friends. We've been speakers and panelists at the same symposiums—Michael representing the farmer, me representing the restaurateur, both of us stressing the connection between the field and the plate. I've seen his work as a farmer and as a teacher, and he does both with passionate conviction. But through this book I've come to know Michael and the farm in a new and more intimate way. I see now how his philosophy about good food and responsible agriculture took shape in the daily struggle to keep one small farm alive and flourishing.

Fairview Gardens is a storybook farm set right in the middle of generic suburban sprawl—surrounded, but not swallowed up, by the banal urbanization that has destroyed so much of California farmland. Its continued existence demonstrates that there may yet be hope, even in the midst of strip malls and fast food joints: hope for slow food and all that ought to imply—grown organically by people who live and work nearby; food you can buy directly from the grower; food that will be prepared, served, and shared by families and friends.

Fairview Gardens is inspirational to me because just as Michael has refused to let the farm be destroyed by urbanization, he has refused to let his voice be drowned out by the incessant, seductive voices advertising artificial food. Michael knows first hand both the environmental wisdom and the cultural benefits of small scale, diversified agriculture, and he has devoted himself to demonstrating the linkages, both practical and spiritual, that connect the good table to the good earth.

This book offers a glimpse into the lessons provided by Fairview Gardens, as well as a great deal of practical knowledge required to farm well. It offers the humble reminder that good food starts in fields and orchards well tended. This is knowledge that we ignore at our peril, for without good farming there can be no good food; and without good food there can be no good life.

Preface

Tract home developments with names such as New Horizons and Village Terrace are bordered and connected by Kings Way, Via Fiori and Fairview Avenue—the corridors of suburbia running east-west and north-south across the Goleta valley. From the air, this area is a vast, gray, gridlike expanse with one strange exception: a small green oasis. Dotted with orchards and lined with field crops, it forms a different pattern, less linear, more undulating. From the ground the image clarifies into avocados and peaches, peppers and tomatoes, cherimoya and mulberry trees, surrounded by gas stations, fast food restaurants, shopping centers, and Highway 101 in a straight shot ninety-nine miles to Los Angeles.

Fairview Gardens was not always an urban farm. Two centuries ago, it was a tiny corner of a grand rancho—four thousand acres of pasture land and live oak between the foothills and the Pacific Ocean. Before that, and deep into the past, these twelve verdant acres were part of the largest Chumash Indian settlement on the central coast of California.

When the first plow cut into this land, sometime in the late nineteenth century, the topsoil was thirty feet deep. Goleta was farming country. Fairview Gardens was not the strange sight that it is now. Just fifty years ago, half of America lived on the land, and this was just one small farm among many.

This land has meant different things to different people. For the Chumash, who did not farm, it was an unspoiled homeland; for the Spanish ranchers, a conquest. Turn-of-the-century settlers saw a place to build a home, establish orchards, and hunt in the lush watershed that once thrived here. Now, the remaining twelve acres feeds a growing suburban population, educates their children in the ways of the earth, and provides a place for music and cultural events. This tiny piece of land has also stirred controversy and galvanized a community to save and protect it.

On Good Land is the story of my seventeen years on this farm — one brief and fertile episode in the long history of this land.

Fairview Gardens 1954

Fairview Gardens 1998

1.

Green Peaches and Broken Pipes

I first came to Fairview Gardens to graft orange trees. In 1981 the Goleta Valley had not yet awakened from its agricultural slumber, and the twelve-acre farm on Fairview Avenue was still surrounded by orchards. There were a few indications of what was to come: a small shopping center, two gas stations, a library, and a retirement community. A number of open and fallow fields remained, vulnerable to the frenzy of real estate development that was just getting started.

It was cheap to lease farmland on those doomed fields. The landowners welcomed the short-term farmer tenants, not for the rent they would pay but for the increased water usage they represented. Irrigation smoothed the way for the eventual sale to developers and the requisite zoning changes. Tract homes could always be shown to require less water than farms, and water—or the lack of it—was an overarching concern in this region.

In those days, Fairview Avenue was still like a primary rural road, with little traffic and less activity. Even then, in the relative quiet of preboom Goleta, when I first drove through the library parking lot and up the driveway to the farm, it was like entering another world. The little farm was caught somewhere between a 1960s back-to-the-land commune and the new wave of serious market gardens that was just beginning to change the face of the American food scene.

The turn-of-the-century farmhouse stood gray and dilapidated at the top of a knoll overlooking the fields. There were a few rows of peach trees, a block of young avocado trees, a large orchard of mature avocado trees, a raised-bed vegetable garden, and various haphazard sections of row crops.

Aside from the few naked bodies working in the fields, what first grabbed my attention were the weeds. Not just a few weeds among the crops, but entire fields of weeds. And healthy ones. Huge leaves of malva, wild radish, thistle, and amaranth waved in the breeze with the fearlessness of those that have no natural enemies.

Chris Thompson was running the farm. In my ignorance I questioned his state of mind that he would let these marauders run unchecked, that

he and his naked staff couldn't keep the fields "clean." I was surprised to learn that this was done deliberately. The concept rattled my commonplace assumption that a farm or garden must have straight rows filled only with what we put in them. This was just the first time this little farm would reshape my view of the world.

I followed Chris to my worksite, faintly alarmed as I climbed through the weeds and brush to get to the orange trees. I had come to this place to practice some of my "expertise" and apply my acquired "skill" in the art of plant manipulation. My sense of agricultural omnipotence was already being eroded. Though I had been a so-called organic orchardist for several years, I still viewed agriculture as some sort of race to the harvest between myself and nature. Was it possible that agriculture could be a cooperative venture, one that worked with nature rather than against her?

As I finished making the last cut on the Washington navel graftwood and inserted it into the bark of the rootstock, Chris mentioned that he was considering a leave of absence. Even as my mind was overwhelmed with the wild and overgrown state of this place, there was something about it that spoke to me. It wasn't long before my wife Donna, our infant son

Aaron, and I had moved into the rambling old farmhouse, and Chris began preparing us to farm sit. Chris never did return as manager, and I entered into an agreement with the owners of the farm to take over.

One of the first things I felt compelled to do as manager was to deal with the three-acre overgrown field that bordered Fairview Avenue, the main thoroughfare. Using a well-worn Italian orchard tractor and a rotary mower, I began circling, moving slowly to the center of the field in concentric circles. The low profile tractor hugged the ground and the dry weeds towered above, in some places standing eight feet high. I felt very small and extremely slow as I crept along.

It was a warm day and I remember entering that kind of ethereal state that comes from repetitive action and moving continuously in circles. In my methodical wake, the field was tidy and clipped. Down came giant malva, then burly thistle, then mustard. As each fell, I advanced to conquer the next stand, until there at the center of the field, mowed open and exposed to the world, was a small patch of mature marijuana plants.

Apparently, along with cabbage, carrots, and beets, marijuana had been a reliable crop for my predecessors. I hesitated just for an instant. Down came the marijuana, crushed under the purposeful whir of the mower.

'Ambrosia' cantaloupes are perfectly round and named for their flavor and their melt-in-your-mouth sweet, smooth texture. The field just below the house was littered with them. I remember thinking how easy organic farming was as I made my way through the field filling a two-bushel picking sack to the brim every twenty-five feet. These plants were volunteers; they had sprouted on their own from seeds dropped by last year's crop.

This easy bounty confirmed my belief that aside from going out at night and squashing bugs, organic farming was about throwing the seeds over your shoulder and coming back in a couple of months to harvest. Seventeen years later, I am just beginning to understand the subtleties of

18

knowledge, skill, and patience it takes to farm with nature, and within complex natural systems. I have also learned that on a small, vintage farm, nature is not the only one who builds complex systems.

It was a Saturday afternoon. Donna's family was coming for a visit and I was out trying to control more weeds with the tractor and a disc attached to the hydraulic three-point hitch. As I lifted the disc and spun the tractor around, I managed in one deft move to get an entire irrigation control station of valves and pipes lodged in the disc. With every attempt to free things up the tangle grew worse until pipes began breaking. This was not simply a case of breaking a few small-diameter PVC pipes; this was a full-scale disaster involving mangled two-inch galvanized pipes, broken valves, breaks below ground, and fountains of water. Chris had neglected to advise me of the location of the main water shutoff and I had forgotten to ask. By the time I located it, the tractor was sinking in the mud, the pipes were still intertwined with the disc, it was Saturday evening with the plumbing supply stores closed, and my mother-in-law was about to arrive.

This was, in a manner of speaking, my baptism and the first and most inconvenient of our plumbing mishaps, but it was not the last. Such problems were inevitable. Beneath the hundred-year-old farm was a labyrinth of water pipes. Some were new, but most remained as a time-line of the agricultural history of this valley, a saga of boom crops that had come and gone—walnuts, then lemons, then avocados—each crop requiring a new or updated irrigation system.

I imagined the Goleta Valley from the view of a gopher, like some massive underground network of cement, galvanized, and PVC highways. Fairview's own tangled irrigation history, consisting of some thirty different systems throughout the farm, was just one messy cloverleaf. There was no official map. The eleven-by-fourteen-inch piece of cardboard with the basic mainlines drawn on it was rained on so often it looked like all the water systems had burst and bled into one.

Eventually, the tractor found each and every pipe. My plumbing

How to Pick a Peach

Harvesting fruit requires sensitivity, acute observation, and patience. Before picking a peach, try to be aware of all of your senses. Imagine that eating the fruit begins with seeing the whole tree, discerning its parts, and visually consuming its shapes and colors. Try to smell for ripeness and allow your eyes to land on the fruit that calls to you in its readiness. Without touching, look closely at its color, at the exposed side and then the unexposed side. Most tree fruit has layers of skin color. Beneath the more obvious reds of an apple, for example, are various shades of green or yellow. These are called the ground or base colors. If the ground color of the peach is mostly pale yellow and the body of the fruit red or orange it is probably close. Carefully, using the palm of your hand, cradle the fruit and move it gently. If after vigorous movement it refuses to let go, move on. If it comes off easily in your hand it is ready.

Eat slowly.

skills improved immensely during that first year. But it wasn't just broken irrigation lines that inspired ingenuity. The farm equipment I inherited was a motley collection, including an old grain drill, a single shank subsoiler with metal wheels, and a sickle bar mower that was set up to be drawn by a horse. With some of this antique equipment, I spent as much time repairing as using the tool.

My career as a farmer has been intertwined with old machinery and I came to believe that along with regular maintenance, machines want respect. The ritual of starting the 1968 Dodge farm truck was always preceded with a moment or two of silence, an appeal to the spirit of the machine. The Italian orchard tractor demanded constant devotional offerings of spare parts shipped from the homeland. The old manure spreader that I received as a gift required a full-time mechanic for its part-time use.

For many years, I used a mechanical sprayer from the 1940s to apply an organic foliar fertilizer on the orchards and to spray minerals on the peach trees to control leaf curl. It took two people all day to spray a couple of acres. Even with constant fiddling, the engine would shut off at regular intervals. Restarting required the two of us to stand over it like faith healers, praying it would start with the next arm-wrenching pull of the starter. The sprayer's pump was a piece of mechanical sculpture: brass fittings and pistons churning up and down in an automated slam dance. Occasionally the rhythm was interrupted by pressure surges that burst the hose, dowsing sprayer and operator with concentrated seaweed and liquid fish emulsion. Then, reeking of pureed fish and seaweed, it was off to the local hardware store for repair parts.

In 1987, we purchased my dream machine, a brand new concentrate blower sprayer, with a high velocity fan that allowed us to drive the tractor down the rows of trees, spraying as we went. What used to take days to accomplish could be done in half an hour. Even so, there was something about the old process that I missed, as direct interaction with the trees was replaced by this more modern, more removed, less fragrant technology.

23

I first arrived at the farm in late July, just after the peach harvest, and happily gorged myself on the gleanings that had been left on the trees. They were incredible, juicy, dead ripe, and as sweet as could be. Swept away by the flavor, I decided to expand the peach orchard. Like a lovesick suitor deciding to marry a few nights into the courtship, I set the farm's direction based on my intoxication with a few tree-ripe gleanings.

I also wanted to build on the novelty of growing organic peaches on the coast in a challenging climate. Most fruit trees require winter chilling for an appropriate dormancy and subsequent leaf and fruit production, but our climate has famously mild winters. I ordered hundreds of peach trees, most of them a variety called 'August Pride.' It never occurred to me to wonder why Fairview's peach harvest had been over in July.

With a few friends, Donna and I began the process of converting some of the lower fields into orchard. We worked the soil deeply and planted cover crops to provide a healthy foundation for the new planting. We designed and installed new irrigation systems, composted, marked the rows, and drilled holes for the trees. The two-man post hole digger occasionally caught on a rock or a root and sent us flying.

The prospect of a new orchard brings a sense of responsibility; it's like starting a new family. I find myself reflecting on the future when I plant a tree. Each planting is an unspoken contract that ties me closer to the land—will I be here to prune, to weed, to compost, to nurture it over the years to fruition?

When the planting stock arrived, we had big tree-planting parties, and I ran around frantically checking everybody's work. Were the eager, less experienced tree planters setting the bareroot, half-inch diameter sticks at the right depth? Was the soil lightly tamped back around the roots with no air spaces? Was the chicken wire that lined each hole to protect the young tree from gophers in place? Once they were in the ground, we hand-watered the trees with buckets, positioned irrigation lines, and pruned each tree to approximately thirty-six inches high.

I was fanatical then, concerned about every detail. In my own relentless way I had the right idea. Through twenty-two years of experience, I have come to know that good farming is not so much about the broad strokes and big ideas. It grows from the confluence of millions of details.

The new orchard leafed out that spring. At the same time, the two rows of older trees flowered and set fruit. It was a large crop that year and because peach trees tend to set fruit on every flower, two of us spent a couple of weeks thinning. Thinning has always been a favorite job as it allows time for the mind and mouth to wander. The hands can move unconsciously down each branch, leaving the superior fruit spaced every eight inches. Almost mindless work, it provides great opportunity for joking, chattering, and thinking.

For the novice and fainthearted it is difficult to remove 90 percent of the crop the tree has set and leave the ground covered with hundreds of little peaches. But to discover a forgotten branch at harvest time loaded with small, inferior, poorer tasting fruit, while the thinned branches are weighed down with large, colorful, flavorful peaches, is to understand the importance of this task. It always seems that the apple is a wiser species because it has the good sense to self-thin some of its crop.

That first season, with hopes high, I made daily visits to the orchard to check the size, moisture, insect damage, and evolution of the crop. When harvest time came at the peak of one of our foggy summer spells, the greenish yellow color of the fruit was not taking on any of that wonderful red and orange blush people expect in a peach. I began to worry. The fruit, to my dismay, tasted sweet and delicious. When it began dropping it was clear that, green as it looked, this variety was in fact ripe. The peach crop had to be harvested or lost.

We began the harvest using an old trailer with a mounted umbrella as a mobile packing station, pulling it down the rows of the trees where the pickers exchanged full buckets for empty ones. Peach by peach, the packing crew sorted the fruit by size into boxes, scrambling to keep up with the pickers. At the end of each day, the overloaded trailer was pulled

back to the house, and the boxes of fruit stacked into the old converted milk truck we were using for a cooler.

At that time, there were only a handful of organic peach growers in the entire state of California and our fruit came on at a time when no one else had much. The wholesaler in San Francisco was happy to buy from us. Happy, that is, until the shipment arrived. Then came the phone calls. The complaints started dropping like the fruit off the trees: "No color; too green; too yellow; too fragile; bruise too easily. We can't sell them." They agreed with me on how good they tasted, but shippability, color, and durability were more important. The old milk truck was now so full that behind the door was a wall of green peaches from floor to ceiling, with no way even to walk in.

Though I tried everything to improve what was fundamentally the wrong variety, things only got worse. Each successive year brought a new way of handling the fruit. I decided to pick as ripe as possible, just before the fruit would go soft. I expounded on the imperceptible changes from light green to not-so-light green, and did fingernail checks on my harvest crew each day, spotting long nails that would slice the delicate fruit. Cotton gloves were issued for picking, picking containers were lined with special foam, and the fruit packed in special single-layer boxes. By now, with the newer trees bearing, it took two full days to get through the first harvest pass and the next pass had to start immediately. A hot spell at the peak and I'd wake up in the night to the sound of ripe fruit dropping.

The irony of it all was that the fruit tasted sublime. At the farmers' market we cut samples, and every person who tasted bought fruit. The market management soon decreed that we couldn't offer samples—it was against health regulations. No samples meant no sales, so we began to sneak slices to willing takers, as if green peaches were some sort of controlled substance.

Finally, facing mountains of ripe fruit, I made an arrangement with an apricot ranch in the inland Ojai Valley to use their drying racks.

28

Goleta's coastal climate was not hot enough or predictable enough for sun drying fruit. We loaded up several thousand pounds of peaches on my old military-issue Dodge Power Wagon, piled six people into the crew cab, and made our way slowly to the Halls' ranch a few hours away.

The ranch had a cutting shed with stacks of old wooden racks surrounding it. Forming an assembly line, we halved the peaches, pulled the pits, and laid the fruit cut side up on the racks. When each rack was covered, we placed it on a light gauge rail car parked in the shed. When the car was loaded with racks, it rolled on the rails out to an open field, where the racks were carefully stacked in the sun. Temperatures frequently reached 110 degrees out there, and I was sure that when I listened carefully I could hear the open flesh of that fruit singe. Within hours the flesh would seal and within a few days the fruit was fully dry. It is amazing how several thousand pounds of fruit—a full, overloaded truck—converts to a dozen medium-sized boxes when dry.

The flavor was rich and smoky, the texture chewy. Unfortunately, as good as they were, the market for dried peaches was limited. We needed another alternative. I contacted a company that custom packed jams and jellies for private labels, and they worked up a recipe for peach butter. The only problem was that the product had to ship as puree and a commercial puree machine was way beyond our means.

We cleaned up a garbage disposal, mounted it on a wooden frame, rented several two-burner propane stoves and large pots, and created baskets from chicken wire. We filled the wire baskets with ripe peaches, blanched them in boiling water, skinned and pitted them, and pureed them in the garbage disposal directly into a dozen used, fifty-gallon food-grade drums. The drums, we discovered on delivery, had been previously used for jalapeño pepper sauce, so it was a job to clean them. To this day, twelve years later, you can still smell the peppers in those drums, and their lingering memory surely added to the flavor of our peach butter.

After that year, it was time to diversify. A few peach trees were worth bending over backwards for, but there were many other things we could be growing. We took out much of the original orchard and grafted some of the trees over to plums. Asparagus, apricots, white nectarines, and apples filled in some of the spaces vacated by the peach trees. I hired more crew and began to increase production of annual row crops.

The experiment with growing tree fruit for distant markets was over. Instead, we would provide the expanding community around us with a continuous supply of French beans, broccoli, peas, lettuce, melons, tomatoes, potatoes, carrots, beets, peppers, corn, squash, and artichokes. With that decision I unknowingly set Fairview Gardens on the road to its future.

2.

Walking the Land

For me, farming was like falling in love. Both are means of perpetuating the human species. My relationship with the land followed a classic course. Nature seduced me and I fell in love with the little farm on Fairview Avenue. I was in awe of the magic of emerging seeds, and enchanted by early morning harvests when beads of dew formed on taut squeaky cabbages reflecting the light of the world.

At some point, like all lovers, I fell out of love in the purely romantic sense of the word. When that intoxicating, blinding draw faded, a deeper relationship began.

I came to farming without training, academic credentials, books, or expectations. My grandparents had farmed but not my parents. I thought technique was important. I thought I should become masterful. Over time I discovered that it was more important to learn how to see.

My best agricultural practice was to walk the fields and orchards, observing, taking notes, poking, digging, smelling, and inspecting. Everyday was different, sometimes dramatically so. Usually the changes were nearly imperceptible. But there were always changes. Some came directly from nature. A sudden heat spell made tiny green beans grow to harvest size in a matter of hours. In the waxing cycle of the moon, seeds germinated almost overnight; in the waning cycle, roots strengthened and took hold.

Sometimes the changes resulted directly from my own actions. If I cultivated the lettuce or brassicas, they seemed to double in size within days. Fruit trees responded to compost or pruning. By trial and error I learned and relearned until the technique I aspired to was internalized and forgotten, as technique should be. I also learned its limits, and how difficult it is to outsmart nature. Farmers are eternally optimistic in this respect, as we try to ripen pumpkins just in time for Halloween, have the first tomatoes at the farmers' market, or grow tender salad greens among much stronger native weeds.

Within a few years of arriving at Fairview Gardens, I went from being a struggling peach farmer to a kind of ringmaster. When I decided to reduce the emphasis on peaches and turn Fairview Gardens into an all-purpose cornucopia, I couldn't stop. Soon Donna and I and the small crew were learning how to best irrigate peppers, sow corn, and hill up potatoes. The catalogs that came from Stokes or Johnny's or Abundant Life tempted me to experiment with nearly twenty-five different tomato varieties. The lettuce beds evolved into a mix of baby greens so diverse that when I described them to visitors I felt like a waiter in a fancy restaurant—'Lacinato,' 'Tres Fin Frisee,' and 'Tango' sounded more like exotic sauces than simple salad greens.

I discovered the treasure hunt pleasures of growing potatoes, an invisible crop that at harvest reveals multi-colored tubers of Yukon Gold, Red Pontiac, Sangre, and Yellow Finn. Peppers pushed me to the outer edges of sanity as I insisted on planting every color from golden yellow and lilac purple to chocolate, seeking the super sweet of the small red Lipstick and the dangerous hot of the golden orange Habanero.

When I came, the land was still a relatively empty canvas. Soon we colored in the various unplanted areas, taking advantage of the subtle micro-climates that naturally existed. Mandarin oranges filled in at the highest point in a warm frost-free area; figs and lemons thrived in one of the hottest spots below the compost. Cold-loving apples grew well along the bottom of the land where cool air settles. To create screens from the road and habitat for birds and insects, hedgerows of pomegranate and nectarine went in along the northern border. Blackberry and sycamore filled in along a creek outflow.

The landowner, Dr. Chapman, watched as the peach orchards gave way to a riot of new crops splashed around the land. He must have wondered what I was up to, though he never asked. Certainly this was as far from commercial agriculture as you could get. Instead of fields full of broccoli grown to supply supermarkets by the truck-full, Fairview was becoming a kind of supermarket in itself, diverse and ever changing like an agricultural botanic garden.

Nearly everything I read or heard about I tried. Lettuce went in among the cabbage and carrots among the tomatoes, a companion-planting technique designed to confuse pests and provide complementary growing conditions. Nitrogen-hungry corn followed nitrogen-rich beans. Insects succumbed to a spray made in the kitchen blender from the bodies of the pests themselves. Dr. Chapman, who was a music professor at the University of California, had an academic's nose for experimentation. He soon showed up with suggestions and priorities of his own, some prophetically forward-thinking, some eccentric, shaded by what turned out to be the beginnings of Alzheimer's disease.

It seemed like every conversation with Dr. Chapman in those first few years included mention of the brass doorknobs in the old farmhouse. The house was built in 1895; it needed a new roof, a paint job, a major electrical overhaul, and new plumbing, but Dr. Chapman persistently reminded me to polish the brass doorknobs.

At the same time his understanding of agriculture was far-reaching. He came across like the Peter Sellers character Chauncy Gardener in the film *Being There:* somewhat absent-minded, accidentally wise. His wisdom was hardly accidental. He regularly appeared with books or articles he wanted to discuss on concepts that went far beyond my own thinking at the time. He introduced me to the theories of glaciation, which suggest the use of rock dust as a way to remineralize the soil. He brought texts on traditional agroforestry; he warned of climate change before that concept was popularly accepted. And then talk would return to doorknobs.

The house with the brass doorknobs stands on a little rise shaded by two struggling sycamore trees. In spring, purple blossoms of jacaranda hang over the back door. A wisteria vine drapes across the front porch and winds to the top of the thirty-foot redwood tree. When I first arrived, the kitchen, painted a sickly yellow, had two tiny windows, one of them blocked by a large, leaning barn. I was told it was built by a previous

34

Pruning

Consider not pruning at all. Allow one tree to be wild and compare the results. Read a pruning manual or speak to an "expert" and you will get a different opinion from each and every source. Find your own way. Trees will speak to you if you listen; they will guide your hands and shears.

Some advice anyway. Stand back and see the whole tree. Understand its natural structure before imposing your own. Come to know its variety and what type of wood produces the largest and most delicious fruits. The peach produces the best fruit on the previous year's growth, apples on second and third year wood. Pruning is our way of making the tree young again each year. Remember that light and air are important elements in the health and vitality of a fruit tree and in the quality of its fruit.

Prune to create openness and air movement. Each cut made stimulates a response. If you cut too much the tree will respond with rank and vigorous growth, too little and it will languish and lose vitality. Seek balance.

owner who wanted to hide the view of the mountains from his mother-in-law while she washed dishes.

Eventually I found time to paint, sand the floors, and generally spruce up the house. The old barn was so infested with termites that a screwdriver slid easily into any beam. I hooked a cable to it and with the old blue truck pulled the whole thing down, liberating the ghost of the mother-in-law.

The house became a light and airy home with views of the mountains, fields, and orchards. It also became a gathering place for the farm staff and community, office space, and the center for most events and activities. Private it is not, and from its perch on top of the hill it picks up traffic sound from Highway 101, the local airport, Fairview Avenue, and the school across the street. Leaving the house in the morning I sometimes catch myself marching, keeping time to the rhythm of the drums and cymbals of band practice.

The house has an endless array of visitors, most invited, some not. Occasionally a stray visitor walks in the kitchen door, through the living room, and out onto the front porch. One year, my son's Christmas presents simply disappeared from under the tree. The big dining room table has seen some magnificent meals; it is truly the heart of the home, as it should be. But it has also been headquarters for mailings, sign-making sessions, staff meetings, and the frantic push to finish my first book.

36

From the beginning, the kitchen has always drawn the heaviest traffic, as every gathering, meeting, event, and drop-by visit centers around food. As the fields filled with new crops, more people came to work, or just to eat, and Donna graciously fed every passerby. Mysteriously, people seemed to gather just as food was being served or prepared, and there were whole months when we rarely shared a private meal together. At the

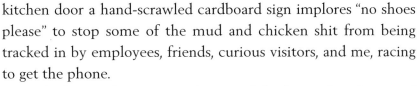

kitchen door a hand-scrawled cardboard sign implores "no shoes please" to stop some of the mud and chicken shit from being tracked in by employees, friends, curious visitors, and me, racing to get the phone.

The human business swirls around the house, but the varied sections of the farm are just as busy and unpredictable, each with unique character and demands. As I make my rounds in the relative quiet of the early morning, a list of tasks forms: restack boxes in the shed, cultivate basil, stop watering the strawberries, repair steering leak on the tractor. This is a dangerous time of the day because this is when new ideas are hatched.

When I first saw the small equipment parking lot next to the house, the soil compacted almost as hard as asphalt, I saw opportunity. Working by myself with a spade, pick, and digging bar, it took three days to dig thirty-six holes. I chose this unlikely site to plant one of my favorite fruits because it was warm and at the top of a hill. Surely with a little care and a lot of cover cropping, composting, and mulch the soil would heal.

Now there are places in that orchard where I can sink my arm in to the ground up to my elbow. Loose and rich, the soil is blanketed with a thick bed of mulch that conserves moisture, controls weeds, and breaks down to create a rich living topsoil, nourishing the thirty-six, droopy-leafed cherimoya trees.

The cherimoya is a heart-shaped subtropical fruit with a light green alligator-like skin. The interior flesh is cream colored, the flavor a smooth blend of mango, banana, peach, pear, and pineapple. The flower is very

On Mulch

Nature is the best recycler. Use her example. Mulching conserves moisture, encourages and increases biological activity in the soil, keeps weeds in balance, and builds soil. Mulch is nature's blanket. Seek out local mulching materials, but don't take leaves from under your trees, robbing them of valuable nutrients. Try noncolored cardboard, old straw or hay, used bedding from livestock, leaves, cuttings, and branches. Go heavy but maintain a buffer zone between mulch and trees and plants. Slugs, snails, and pill bugs like mulch too, but will not cross an area left clear. Come back later, pull back the thick layers you have applied and experience the moisture and rich life you have helped create.

long and there is no insect in this part of the world that has a long enough proboscis to pollinate it, so we have to pollinate by hand. On summer afternoons, we collect pollen from the male flowers in small containers and slip a camel-hair brush loaded with pollen into the female flowers. When it hits the pistil, we gently twist the brush to evenly distribute the pollen. It's as up close and intimate as you can get with any plant.

In orchard years, the cherimoyas are young. By contrast, the grand and stately avocado trees are the old men of the farm. They stand thirty feet tall and spread their limbs to create a large, enclosed, expansive cavern we call the cathedral. One of Fairview's former owners, Mr. Harms, came to visit before he died. He said he had planted the avocado trees in August 1954, the month and year I was born.

Over their forty-four years, these great trees have come to be more like a forest than a commercial orchard. During tours of the farm, we always stop here and sit in a circle in the dappled light. I ask my visitors to close their eyes, cup their hands, and, as if receiving communion, accept some of the moist, rich topsoil scooped up from beneath the trees. Some of them look skeptical or squirm when they encounter an earthworm. "This is where our food comes from," I say, asking them to examine the soil closely and smell it deeply. One pinch of living soil contains millions of forms of life, and the vitality of all living things is directly and inextricably tied to the health of the soil.

This lesson is the most important one for the young people who come to visit here. It was the lesson I learned through years of trial and error.

At first, every time there was a problem with a crop, I searched for reasons and solutions from the outside, as if the world of plants was full of foreign invaders. Later, when I discovered that everything followed from the condition and fertility of the soil, I understood why some cultures call it the earth's placenta. This simple understanding dictates everything I do on this piece of land.

Steve Soderquist arrived one February just in time to help me plant mandarin oranges. He stayed for six years. Steve was the most predictable human being I have ever met, from his morning greeting of "top o' the mornin'" to the food that he ate every day. Breakfast was a few sunflower seeds and some oats; lunch was the previous evening's leftovers of what he called "he-man food": lentils and brown rice stir-fried with a little tamari. Steve was quiet most of the time except for the occasional hyena-like outburst of laughter or strong opinion on immigration or organic agriculture.

He was also one of the few gringos who could hold his own in the fields. There has been a parade of young people through here over the years, eager to work on a farm. Their enthusiasm tempers on the second or third day when they discover that it is repetitious work, that it can be hot or cold or wet, and that one's mind must be dealt with to stay out there and work all day. Learning how to work physically, tame the chatter of the mind, and push through a sore back or a hot day, takes time and perseverance.

Everyone said it was crazy to consider planting mandarins, that it was a waste of time and money, and that it was best to stick with something proven. But no has always meant yes to me. I wanted to stretch the possibilities on this land, secure a stable winter cash crop, and plant something unique.

The standard varieties, such as Dancy and Kara, were already growing locally. I decided on an Algerian variety. The name "Clementine"

40

sounded good, and it was rumored to be popular in Europe, especially in France. This was not the most scientific way to make a thirty-year commitment. These trees would be in the ground three to five years before bearing the first fruit and would live twenty-five to thirty years overall.

The field I had in mind for the mandarins was directly across the driveway from my then two-year-old cherimoyas. It was rich and fertile, so the balled and burlapped young trees went in smoothly. I remember looking over that field of young trees like my granddad used to look over his extended family, with great pride and hope for the future.

A few months later, a neighbor hired the Eager Beaver Tree Company and told them they could drive through our "open field" to trim her pine trees. The Beavers didn't see me frantically waving my arms and screaming as their convoy of trucks and chipping machines rumbled over the newly planted orchard like it was a highway. It had just rained and the weight of those big trucks on the wet ground created deep ruts between the trees. Any trees that were in the way were flattened, and I felt like I had been run over as well. The tree cutters claimed they were just doing their job, the neighbor claimed ignorance, and I won a small settlement in small claims court. This was the first of a number of times when urban and rural conflicts got played out before a judge and an amused courtroom of people.

'Clementines' flower in spring and put out fruit from November to March. After two years of waiting for the first harvest, the fruit tasted terrible. The next year, it was still sour and lacking in any flavor. It seemed that my experimentation and entrepreneurial adventurism were only getting us into trouble. Just when it seemed prudent to graft the trees to another variety, things changed. Like magic, the sugar and flavor of the fruit improved dramatically, and it keeps getting better with every successive season. I now know that until the trees root deep into the ground, the flavor and sugar levels are low. And contrary to the commonly held belief that "fresh off the tree" is always best, this variety improves with age. A few days after harvest that subtle tart flavor turns sweet and rich.

Now, during spring, the first impression of the farm as you come up the driveway from the world of traffic and shopping malls is a blast of fragrant blossoms. In winter, thousands of small bright orange fruits hang against the deep shiny green of the trees, and at the farmers' market our 'Clementines' bring in every French-speaking person for miles around.

One of the ironic challenges of farm life is how to feed the farmer and his family. While I filled Fairview's twelve acres with new plantings, we still needed to eat on a daily basis. We could not wait while orchards matured and came into bearing, or while I developed a working plan for the field crops.

So, in a collection of raised beds bordered by a black mulberry tree and a hedge of pomegranate and carob trees, Donna and I began spending spare moments together growing a kitchen garden. We sprinkled those beds with convenient plantings of lettuce, beets, carrots, radish, beans, and broccoli. Here we also experimented with the rare and unusual, with varieties untested in the larger fields. In that sheltered and quiet garden we could slow down, dig beds by hand, and raise

44

food for the family table. Aaron was just walking then. He toddled naked among the beds, picking up slugs and watering with hose and sprinkler head whenever we let him.

Eventually the kitchen garden became a full-time salad garden and the larger fields filled up with reliable harvests of every kind of fruit and vegetable. We were able to graze nearly the whole farm, snacking on carrots or nectarines, collecting our evening meal on a walk from the salad beds to vast tomato plantings to the asparagus patch, from long rows of basil and peppers in summer or cauliflower and kohlrabi in winter. Every summer evening, dinner included green beans and corn; the artichoke harvest eventually extended until we could eat them every day for months.

It may have seemed like I wanted to domesticate the entire farm, but Fairview retained a wild core. Every farm or garden needs its wild spaces. Within and beneath the mixed stand of pines, oak, and eucalyptus that towers over the center of the farm are rodent-eating owls and beneficial insects that pollinate and protect crop plantings. The shady corridors would eventually become habitat for humans too, a hodgepodge community of trailers, tents, and a Mongolian yurt to house employees and interns and to host the occasional musical gathering around the big fire pit.

The first time I met my employer Cornelia Chapman, she was striding through the grove in a white space suit, gloves, veil, and pith helmet. She carried a smoker, which she used to calm her beehives before harvest. We were more than a generation apart in age and the gulf in our backgrounds was vast. Her father was the founder of the Dutch Shell Oil Company and she grew up with unimaginable wealth. In England during the war, she was a member of The Women's Land Army, traveling from farm to farm filling in for the male farm workers who were off fighting. She was, among other things, a teamster and I have never had trouble imagining her behind a team of draft horses. Her American husband Roger was the dreamer, musician, and thinker; Cornelia was the one who had her hands in the dirt. In addition to keeping the bees, she loved to garden and harvest from the Fairview fields.

Cornelia eventually gave up beekeeping, and John Hayes and I established some new hives from swarms that neighbors asked us to collect. On occasion, if I was out in the orchard working and wanted a snack—or just wanted to show off—I would find a bee cruising with a load of pollen on its legs. I learned to capture the bee in one hand formed into a loose fist that allowed it to crawl through. By the time the bee flew away, two balls of tasty pollen remained in my hand. If I was too cocky and squeezed too tight I got stung in the palm.

Eventually most of the bees perished to foulbrood, a bacterial disease that infects the larvae. With its mild climate, Goleta has many derelict hives and no winter freeze to kill them off or control disease. I was too stubborn to sprinkle the antibiotic terymyacin on our hives to protect them. By the time I realized my mistake it was too late.

If I don't walk the land, I miss things—the chance to head off a disease or to cultivate at just the right moment to insure a bountiful harvest. These walks are a safeguard. They are also a joy when the first tiny plums appear beneath their flower jackets or I discover a thriving volunteer apricot tree, nature's message that this might be the spot for a larger planting. The most satisfying thing, however, is to see the returning tilth and fertility of the land, when I can grab a handful of dark, rich crumbly soil where before the ground had been hard and cloddy.

Long before I arrived at Fairview, the valuable topsoil on the front field had been scraped off and sold. In my first winter I started on its renewal, planting a mix of peas, beans, and vetch that we mow under every year, just as they begin to flower. Legumes such as these fix nitrogen on their roots, and their leaves and stalks provide the essence of good soil—organic matter.

The three-acre front field was, and remains, Fairview's face to the world; many assume it is the entire farm. When the cover crop gets to be about four feet high and taller, we can hear people as they walk by discussing how lazy we are for not controlling the "weeds." I often thought about putting a sign on the road to identify those "weeds" as our most important crop of the year, the one we grow as a gift to nature for the bounty that she provides on that field during the rest of the year.

In time, this field would be filled with successions of corn and gradually an array of crops—in winter, brassicas and lettuces; in spring, onions, beets, and green garlic; in summer, tomatoes, peppers, basil, and eggplant; and in fall, pumpkins, popcorn, and squash. For much of the year, it is bordered along the road with three-hundred-foot beds of flowers—zinnias backed by tall sunflowers.

This field came to epitomize both our struggle and our opportunity. Newer houses stand at one end. At the other end is the public library, where the county prisoners who maintain the grounds sometimes get overzealous with their weed whackers, taking out some of our vegetables. Working the rows just adjacent to the road it seems that I have grown a bumper crop of soda cans, napkins, Taco Bell salsa packets, and hubcaps. Sometimes, teenagers drive by in their parents' cars and yell "dirt farmer" out the window. I must be a strange sight to their suburban eyes, walking among my weeds.

I often sit in my office with all the windows open on hot still nights. Lacewings, ladybugs, beetles, and tiny flies land on the light and the papers while I work. If I walk out into the heart of the orchards, it seems

47

I am a thousand miles away from cars and highways and strip malls, from the hum of frenetic suburban life. But the farm does not have walls and the smells of hamburgers, fries, and tacos waft in from the fast food outlets that are within walking distance. Delta Airline's last flight to San Francisco takes off at nine. The airport and flight path are so close that from anywhere on the land I can wave my flashlight and be seen by passengers in flight.

Walking the perimeters of the farm, I pass my neighbors' illuminated windows, feeling like a voyeur. Families prepare their children for bed, babies cry, the grayish blue glow of television flickers, and students pore over their homework. The farm reveals another reality. Small animals scurry, owls screech, a slight breeze rustles the leaves on the trees. Air temperatures change as I enter and leave different air currents, and smells of citrus and avocado in bloom come into focus and mix with the rich smell of recovering soil.

3.

Bulldozers and Tract Homes

For two months in 1984, unrelenting noise pulsed from huge machines that arrived to remove the last agricultural holding that bordered the farm. For years we had been huddled up next to each other, two small farms standing against the tide of development. Though Fairview had grown and flourished, our neighbor had given in years before. His lemon orchard, now falling to the big steel blade of the bulldozer, was a wild, derelict remnant. The trees were either dead or almost dead. Thorny root suckers grew from the base of the dried-up trunks, and the weeds were tall enough to cover the trees.

A certain beauty emerged from this neglect, as nature reclaimed the land in the years that the orchard was forgotten. Twenty-six acres were regaining their wildness. The land was full of life. Deer, raccoons, possum, hawks, and coyote passed through a bustling society of birds, small rodents, and insects. In the middle of all this, in a small shack invisible for the vines that covered it, my friend Helmut lived like a forest hermit, his world complete with a small pond, office, and outdoor cooking and dining area.

I fought the demise of that land, feeling feeble standing in the city council chambers with a few other locals facing off against the highly paid lawyers for the developers. The story is always the same. Land is a mere commodity to be bought and sold, something to build on, pave over, mine, or drill. We protested the sacrifice of the richest topsoil on the entire west coast. We cited the agricultural history of this valley, our perfect Mediterranean growing climate, the loss of farmland everywhere, and the importance of small farms and local food for our children. Our voices were drowned out by housing statistics, traffic studies, and promises for parks and tennis courts, all supported by sophisticated maps and graphs.

The local newspaper acted as oracle, putting forth headlines on yet-to-be-approved projects as if they were a sure thing. "Progress Hangs Concrete Shroud on Goleta Farm," the paper solemnly confirmed. The neighbor who sold the land was quoted, predicting, "farming is a dying profession." I had to wonder where *his* food came from.

We all hear stories of the greed that undermines our global environment. Until the bulldozers are idling at your back door, it is an intellectual concept. The pain for us was real. For fifty-eight days, an army of three-hundred horsepower caterpillars, carryalls, and dump trucks moved and buried and leveled and graded hundreds of tons of topsoil.

The bone-rattling noise started at seven each morning and didn't stop until evening. Clouds of dust floated into the farm and covered everything. We complained, and the atmosphere of war seemed only to increase. The line was drawn where the lush green of our avocado orchards met the red flags that marked the roads of the new development. But the battle was about more than just noise and dust, and we were losing. With each day the farm was becoming more like an island. All around us, the once fertile and agrarian valley had become a sea of tract homes and shopping centers. The sense of complete isolation was the hardest to take. With this last development, the farm would be surrounded by suburbia. We were now completely out of context.

There were more struggles to come. Contiguous pieces of land cannot be separated so easily. Nature, especially water, does not abide by surveyors' lines and man-made borders. When twenty-six acres are graded, paved, and covered with rooftops, the watershed is concentrated into runoff, and the impact downstream can be disastrous. A cement culvert large enough to walk through appeared, sticking out into the corner of our land, ready for the next big storm. The Texas-based developer wasn't accustomed to young, upstart farmers standing in his way. When I called in the county flood control to find out how he planned to deal with all that drainage being dumped on our land, he was not happy. The issue, if unresolved, threatened to hold up the works.

After long negotiations, the developer was required to dig a drainage ditch along the bottom of our land and pay the Chapmans thirty-thousand dollars. He planned to make back some of his money by selling the valuable topsoil he dug out of the farm. I stopped him, and the topsoil became a small mountain that we still draw from for compost. The ditch,

How to Fight City Hall

Choose your battles well. There is no point in launching a fight over some minor matter. Pay your parking tickets, but fight like hell if your land is under threat, if your local farmers' market is being moved or closed, or the open wild land next door is proposed for two hundred condominiums. Involve your friends and neighbors. Get them to write letters or load them into the back of your dumptruck (don't get a ticket on the way) to get them down to any hearings or protests. Most importantly, get the local media involved. Find someone at the local newspaper to take an interest in your story. When you are interviewed, keep to the subject and spell it out clearly, but keep in mind that rarely is anything ever reported accurately. Be respectful of your opponent.

purportedly designed to withstand the "hundred-year flood," has flooded into our fields and orchards three of the last six years.

Despite the obstacles we raised, the land next door was subdued, and nature was more or less contained. Construction began and several hundred look-alike tract-home condominiums popped up on the Mars-like landscape. They were given names such as Village Terrace. Unlike any village I have ever visited, they lack any commons, and any real sense of identity or place. The developers who designed and built those homes did not concern themselves with incorporating elements of nature, with creating space for children to play, or with providing for community interaction. The automobile proved to be the most important design priority as most of the open space was given over to roads and driveways.

Then, as if they had been waiting in line at the gates of this new "village," the moving vans arrived. There was a waiting list of ready buyers. With the influx of new neighbors came the beginnings of complaints—about the signs outside our produce stand, the compost, and finally the crow of our roosters.

One of my new neighbors had been a tight end for an NFL football team. He stood about six feet tall and weighed close to two hundred pounds. One evening as the produce stand was closing, he rushed in unannounced and angry. The newly built home he had just purchased was near our compost piles. He wanted the piles removed.

This neighbor filed his complaint with the county health department. They issued an official order for me to "cease and desist" composting. The penalty for non-compliance was jail. I ignored the order. Compost was not just a central part of our natural soil fertility program; it also allowed us to recycle hundreds of tons of green waste that would otherwise clog the local landfills.

We had some explaining to do. Donna and I invited all of our new neighbors over to discuss composting and other issues. Over a home-grown

53

meal of sweet corn, green beans, vine-ripe tomato salad, and fresh baked bread, we talked things through. Most of the neighbors showed up, except for the one who complained so bitterly. He sent his wife.

Exactly one year later, a uniformed county officer was tramping purposely through the peach orchard, her shiny boots threatening the tender celery transplants we had just placed between the rows of trees. "PUBLIC NUISANCE" was printed in bold capital letters on the top of her six-page document. The "ORDER" commanded me to restrict this nuisance, and deemed me responsible for enforcement costs. If I did not comply, the matter would be turned over to the district attorney.

The public nuisance was my roosters. These roosters had run free for many years, fulfilling their part in the balance of the farm, and crowing about it most mornings. When I refused to sign the document, the officer stood bewildered at first, then became angry.

"You'll go to jail if you don't sign," she said with the absolute conviction of a person who knows the law. I refused again, as I refused in prior years to cease and desist composting, or to remove the signs advertising our fresh fruits and vegetables. I refused for reasons that were purely practical to the operation of the farm, and for deeper reasons that involved my principles and convictions. I also felt a responsibility to the community that supports and benefits from the farm.

Soon Fairview Gardens was caught in the eye of a major local controversy heralded by headlines reading "Rooster Riots," "As the Cock Crows," and "Roosters Reveille Stirs Flap." Television crews waited outside

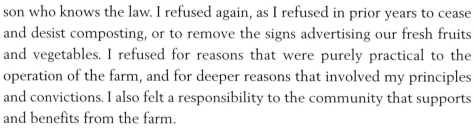

54

the house. Local radio stations set up recording devices to capture the offending noise on tape, and the newspaper assigned a reporter to cover the daily developments. Televised hearings were scheduled and a throng of community supporters of the farm showed up in pop-up rooster hats. Marriages were strained as couples living near the farm were divided on

whether the sound was a nuisance or actually a pleasant background to a suburban environment.

Mail and messages poured in from well-wishers, as well as plenty of expert advice. "Put a large metal bucket over their heads and they can't stretch their necks to crow." "Send them on a flight to Australia and back again to upset their internal time clock." At the county hearing, officials suggested in all earnestness that we cut the vocal cords of the offending beasts.

I responded with an editorial that ran in the local newspaper on

Mother's Day about the archetypal cry of the rooster and our lost connection to the land. Perhaps the district attorney didn't want to take on Mother's Day, the American farm, and a public dressed in rooster hats. Perhaps the public outcry had actually been heard and heeded. Whatever the reason, the district attorney withdrew his charges and the county backed down.

But the issue was not as the media presented it—just about roosters. Nor was the real issue the previous year just about compost. Seen as isolated occurrences, those situations appeared ridiculous, my attitude simply stubborn and uncompromising. The real story had to do with the loss of our relation to the natural world. The crow of the rooster is symbolic. It has been the call of natural rhythm since the beginnings of recorded history. That people wanted to silence that sound was also symbolic. It was one of the last natural sounds left in this valley, even though it could barely be heard over the constant hum of Highway 101 and the roar of jet planes from the nearby airport.

In the years that followed, we spent an inordinate amount of time defending our right to be. An anonymous complaint from a neighbor cost the farm thousands of dollars in conditional-use permits for the fruit stand and a trailer. Both had been on the property for a very long time. Then came theft and vandalism to the produce stand, increased traffic and noise, bottles and trash thrown into the fields, and neighbors' dogs going after our goats, chickens, and a rabbit called Blossom.

The internal battle that raged inside me swung to extremes. I considered holing up on the farm, building fences, guarding our borders, acting as if an alien force had surrounded us. I could keep fighting or begin to educate. I chose the latter. The neighborhood was changing—it was time to change the goals of the farm.

People were beginning to think about food in a new way. Food safety issues were surfacing in the media, as were environmental issues about agriculture. After decades of suburban expansion, people were looking to rediscover their relationship to the land. Parents and teachers wanted new

ways to educate their children. Reaching people through their kids and their stomachs seemed the most powerful and direct approach.

I continued to struggle with bottles in the fields, restricted tractor hours, and dogs chasing livestock. At the same time, my new neighbors were tentatively drifting into the produce stand. At first it was just to pick up the head of lettuce they had forgotten at the supermarket; we were in effect a convenience store. The connection grew gradually as they learned to savor our corn and strawberries, slowly realizing that what the sign said was true: "We Grow What We Sell."

Together we were figuring out what a farm could mean to a suburban population. We were just beginning to recognize how important it could be for our children. Thrown into public discourse over compost and roosters, caught in a collision of urban and rural, we were given the chance to play out and resolve the same issues that were forcing small farms all over this country to shut down.

While the grownups were busy working out the complaints, the kids had already moved in. I discovered secret forts built into the avocado orchard. I found a little plastic table and chairs in a hidden corner of the fields, the setting for carefully planned doll tea parties with muffins and orange juice. Occasionally I was invited to attend.

The hostesses, Sara and Jenny, were just moments away from being too old for dolls. On the farm they clung to the ritual a little longer, even

60

as they haunted the fields asking a million agricultural questions of my crew or searched the underbrush for signs of wild rabbits. For them the farm was full of mystery, and their carefully made notes and totems were left behind, like clues in a treasure hunt. Little brothers came along too, arriving on their motorcross bikes, jumping the curb that separated the farm from the neighboring development, and wiping out into the soft mountain of topsoil we had recovered from the clutches of the developer.

Things quieted down after the rooster riots, maybe because many of those who complained came to understand, even believe in, what we were doing. Or maybe it was because they decided that we were a formidable

foe. One neighbor, whose home borders the long field at the bottom of the property, often left messages saying he would rather look over his fence at condominiums, or that the dust from the tractor was ruining the plaster in his pool. He was most sensitive about the old spreader truck I used to spread compost on the fields. The truck has a big bed with high sides. A belly chain runs along the bed dropping compost into two spinning fans that throw it onto the field about twenty feet to each side of the truck. I could see why this made him nervous.

In the spirit of peaceful co-existence—even harmony—I had a plan. When I needed to spread compost on the lower field, I decided that it would be better for our relationship if it was done before five o'clock, before he came home from work. Unfortunately, one afternoon just as the truck moved into the field, it bogged down and stopped running. It took the rest of the day to get it restarted. By that time, my neighbor was standing at the fence, arms crossed, just waiting for me to make a wrong move.

As I drove along the field near his place, I took extra precautions, veering way off to the side to be sure that the material would not land

61

anywhere near his place. Looking in the mirror, I could see him wave, smile, and acknowledge my careful consideration. I turned around to make another pass, this time on the other side of the field. Just as the truck lined up with his home, a small rock landed on the spinners and was flung like a rocket clear across the field, over the fence, and through his dining room window. There is no way I could have achieved such precision even if I planned it, but his smile faded, as I knew it would.

Peace is never perfect. Sometimes it's little more than a cease fire. I'm sure my neighbor wonders to this day how I got the nerve (or the skill) to pull a stunt like that on purpose. I'm also sure that long after the window was fixed, he enjoyed being left with an indignant story to tell about a reckless, lunatic farmer shooting projectiles with a compost truck.

4.

Of Nubians, Australorps, and Chinese Weeders

One hundred and twenty chickens, three goats, one part-time horse, five hundred thousand bees, three cats, one turkey, six geese, one occasional peacock, seven ducks, a visiting cockateel, between two and thirty-two rabbits, and seventeen humans share Fairview Gardens' 12.23 acres.

The chickens are Australorp, Arucana, Buff Orpington, Polish, Barred Rock, Blue Cochen, and Rhode Island Red, and come in shapes, colors, and sizes as varied as their names. The Himalayan cat, Chinese weeder geese, Nubian goats, and New Zealand white rabbits blend in multicultural camaraderie with Russian, Mexican, French, Italian, and Czechoslovakian humans.

We're an odd mix of domesticated creatures. It's as if we have all been put together in a bizarre, poorly funded experiment in social and ecological dynamics. I like to think that each creature has its logical and preordained place in the workings of the farm. But beyond eating insects, providing fertilizer, controlling weeds, and producing milk and eggs, many are here just to provide love, companionship, comedy, and the occasional tragedy.

It probably reflects some deep-seated prejudice, but I often view farm animals as important only if they provide some "useful" work or product. It's hard to rationalize the tons of feed we buy any other way. The bills from Island Seed and Feed are calculated against eggs laid, gallons milked, and tons of manure produced. All of us here must earn our keep.

With this in mind, I often judge our farm animals by the quantity and particular qualities of their shit. Horseshit is a wonderful soil condi-

64

tioner, pleasant in smell; goats produce a tidy and easy-to-handle manure which contains few if any weed seeds; chicken droppings are high in plant nutrients but difficult to handle. One advantage of raising chickens "free range" is that each one becomes a self-operating mini manure spreader. Uncaged for most of the day, they have acres of open ground to make their deposits on, yet one or two always seem to end up fertilizing the

concrete on my doorstep. There are few things more unpleasant than walking outside in clean stocking feet to grab a shirt out of the back porch laundry and sliding on fresh chicken shit. This inevitably happens when I am on my way to some meeting or social event.

Even so, I firmly believe in "free range." The alternative is the life sentence that most chickens endure in prison-style egg factories where they live in two-by-two-foot cages, their feet hobbled and their beaks cut, with the lights on twenty-four hours a day. While our chickens do leave the occasional inconvenient specimen and have been known to chow down on a young lettuce crop, they are welcome to the full run of our twelve acres.

The truth is they live like royalty. Guests who come for a meal are appalled to see the quality and volume of leftovers we send to the chickens. We only eat the pure white tender hearts of the romaine lettuce and discard the outer leaves; most fruits and vegetables are tossed after a day. When my friend and chef extraordinaire Alice Waters came to visit last Christmas and made mushroom ravioli and Portuguese peasant soup with braised baby leeks, the leftovers were served to our gourmet flock.

"How can you throw that away?" people always ask. But nothing is ever really thrown away. The kitchen scraps end up on top of the newest working compost pile just across from the chicken coop, and the birds have first access to it. As a result, anyone who approaches the coop (especially carrying a bucket) is faced with 120 chickens bearing down on them in a mad stampede, each trying to be the first to partake of the delivery.

For most of the day, they live in pastoral calm, rambling the orchards in couples and small groups in search of bugs, worms, and minerals in the soil. Out under the avocado and peach trees, the flock provides its best service to the soil. I am certain that the action of the chickens constantly scratching the surface of the farm stimulates the land like some giant massage.

To further harness chicken-enhanced fertility, my friend Doug Wade helped me design and build a "chicken tractor" in exchange for a lifetime supply of eggs. Built like a giant rickshaw, this mobile coop allowed the chickens to work the entire farm. The coop, which is their shelter for the night, is about twelve feet long with poles that double as roosts sticking out each end. About one night a month, four of us grabbed a pole, lifted the entire coop full of squawking chickens into the air, and marched like a royal procession to the next location.

We don't move the chickens anymore. They are permanently stationed within easy reach of the compost where they work the piles, keeping them free of fly larvae. During the day they wander where they please, but at night we round them up by bribing them with grain. The call of "Here, chick, chick, chick" brings them racing from the four corners of the farm, to surround whoever is doing the feeding. Jumping over and on top of each other, they scramble for the corn and wheat scattered in the dust around their coop. They don't even notice us closing the gate. Locking them in the coop insures the hens will lay their eggs in the laying boxes, and it keeps them safe—almost—from predators. Occasionally, when they develop a taste for lettuce, or start wandering into the road, we have to enforce a chicken lockdown. After a few days of confinement they forget their bad habits. Chickens have very short memories.

Predators, on the other hand, never forget a food source.

Fairview is an intensive living island jammed with fruits, vegetables, and small helpless animals, floating in the midst of acres of pavement and houses. The farm is a favorite hunting ground for hungry creatures seeking refuge from the ever-expanding suburban control of nature. The chickens feed on weeds and insects, and they in turn exist within a bigger food chain of coyotes, raccoons, and hawks.

One summer morning, my sister who was visiting from New York City, went out to collect the eggs. She returned to the house, pale and shaken. The headless remains of eight chickens had been waiting for her in the coop. A raccoon had reached through the wire and pulled off the heads, with little more trouble than it took my sister to reach into the coop for the eggs.

As a kid, geese always frightened me. Other than watchdog replacements, what role did they play? Then one day I saw a photograph of a man herding geese in his strawberry fields; the caption suggested they were controlling weeds. That's all I had to know. After extensive research (which amounted to a three-minute call to my friend Phil at the feed store to see if he had a goose source) I decided that Chinese weeder geese would work for us. "Raise them on a diet of the weeds you want them to eat," I was told. "And when they grow up they'll keep the fields clean."

It wasn't so simple.

The six-day-old goslings arrived fuzzy yellow with white heads and the beginnings of orange bills. It seemed like they doubled in size each day. To "train" them, we handled them constantly, hand-feeding with malva and wild radish—two of the weeds we wanted them to eat later. Before long they looked like real geese, big and mean, just like I remembered. It became clear that any herding would be determined by their instincts and not our agricultural needs. If we did manage to direct them into the row crops, they ate the cultivated plants instead

69

of the weeds. I still don't know what the man-in-the-picture's secret was.

Soon the only herding we did consisted of moving them away from the fields and keeping them in the main area of the farm near the houses, office, and shops. Here they could be under constant supervision and, unfortunately, within constant earshot. Quiet conversations were now a thing of the past; even the tersest communication turned into a shouting match. The geese felt it was not only their duty to be present at every meeting, but to squawk throughout any exchange, as if voice-activated.

I went down to the local hardware store to buy a kiddie pool, hoping to keep them occupied for at least part of each day. "This one comes with a slide," the helpful salesman pointed out. "Or perhaps you would prefer the one with dolphins printed on the outside? How many children will use this pool?"

We placed the pool within view of the kitchen window and although we changed the water frequently, it seemed like it only took a day before it turned to green scum.

The geese were friendly enough, but nothing seemed to quiet their constant squawking or relieve their need to be huddled up to any flock of humans. The expression "what's good for the goose is good for the gander" started to turn up in conversation. Several of my female friends suggested that maybe these geese needed a gander to keep them company. When the chorus of "get a gander" got as loud as the geese themselves, it was time to act.

He arrived as a day-old, and it was some time before he was well developed enough to assert his role. Things got worse. The geese turned mean. The gander's influence seemed to turn a whole group of loud geese into a whole group of attack geese. They kept away the mailman, frightened off the schoolchildren, and kept visitors safely locked in their cars.

Everyone on the farm learned the art of goose self defense. The trick was to wait until the goose was stretched out in a straight line from beak to belly in attack mode, then just before she lunged, gently grab her long

neck and carefully swing her around to face in the opposite direction. This would so disorient the goose that she would forget who she was attacking and walk away.

One day I accidentally ran over one with my truck. The following week another one was disemboweled by a red-tailed hawk. I was fed up with goose neuroses and couldn't handle any more tragedy. So I packed four live geese and a gander into banana boxes and released them at the man-made lake nearby. Occasionally I ride my bike down to the lake and from a distance watch as small crowds of visitors enjoy the antics of our ex-geese.

Our small flock of turkeys was less fortunate. I have always believed that one should be directly and intimately involved with everything one eats. Thanksgiving was always a dilemma. Although I had vegetarian leanings, once a year I enjoyed slipping into a tryptophane slumber after gorging myself on turkey. I always came away from the table feeling I had avoided a key part of the process. If I couldn't raise and butcher the birds, I probably shouldn't be eating them.

It was time to come to terms with my turkey craving. I bought six turkey chicks with the hope of raising a few additional for some friends. I began eight months in advance to prepare for Thanksgiving dinner.

I had heard all the stories about turkeys, about how stupid and help-less they were, that they were so completely domesticated that they could hardly walk or stand for the bred-in weight of their breast. I was con-vinced that our turkeys would be raised with respect, that intelligence was a matter of perspective, and that come next Thanksgiving the turkeys and I would have worked out the killing thing.

The killing thing never happened, nor did we have our own turkey for Thanksgiving. All but one drowned in the kiddie pool set up for the geese. I found them floating in the shallow water looking like a cult-style mass suicide. One turkey stood quietly by, the sole survivor. We honored

72

her with two names—Ishi, the last of her tribe and Einstein, for her superior intelligence. Einstein has not only lived through six Thanksgivings; she has survived a coyote attack, illness, insults, and two husbands—her first, a tom turkey; her second, a small white duck.

Milky Way lived up to her name. She regularly produced just under a gallon of rich milk a day, more than any other goat we had ever had. Through her efforts, there was enough milk to drink, make cheese, and sell fresh. She came to us on the first day of a farm live-in program for my son's third grade class. I wanted the kids to learn how to milk and Milky Way—as my son named her—arrived udders full and ready to go. She would stand still, her head turned calmly, as she patiently watched twenty excited eight-year-old kids try milking for the first time—grabbing, fumbling, squeezing, and pulling her teats.

Goats, especially Nubians, are sociable creatures. Milky Way has had various companions, including her own offspring—Brownie, Sugar, and Midnight—as well as Painted Chief the horse who oversees the big goat pen and his "girls." The goats spend much of the day sleeping back to back in the dusty potholes they have dug for themselves. When they were young they galloped through the pen, hopping with all four feet off the ground. This cavorting—a goat's ode to joy—often inspired their more sedate mother to rear up on hind legs, head cocked, to join in the action. When anyone approaches the pen the goat family jockeys for position at the fence, necks outstretched, lips flapping in desperation to grasp weeds from outstretched hands. As if we were starving them to death.

No goat has ever starved to death. In fact they are more likely to eat themselves sick, especially if they get into the grain bin. We manage to keep them away from the grain, but we cannot fully protect them from predators, illness, and bad luck.

Midnight died in my arms, just a few weeks old. Jet black except for a small stripe of white on each of her ears, she was a dramatic contrast to her brown and white sister, in fact to any other goat we have ever had. She followed me around like a little dog, her long ears nearly dragging on the ground. It is the best policy not to get too attached to farm animals. I knew better than to make an exception with Midnight, so I guess I deserved my broken heart.

Even in a healthy environment, farm animals occasionally get sick, and sometimes they die. I should have been prepared for what happened when I left a friend to house-sit. I explained nothing to her, except not to wear her shoes in the house, gently suggesting that her urban issue pumps might be swapped for something with a lower profile. A true city girl, she had just returned to America from years living in Tokyo, but I wasn't worried. The crew would take care of the farm; she was just there to feed the cats.

The week before, Milky Way had delivered the year's baby, a boy goat we named Mars Bars. When I left he was in perfect health. The next day Mars stopped nursing.

My friend knew she was not supposed to let the cats or the house-plants die, and she assumed this responsibility extended to newborn goats. I returned to a whopping vet bill for antibiotics and special visits. She proudly explained the lengths she had gone to for this goat. I could picture her in her unsensible shoes, straddling Mars Bars, holding his head back, and pouring warm milk down his throat with a catsup squeezer. She administered the costly intramuscular antibiotic shots twice a day. At night she brought Mars into the kitchen and slept next to him so that when he woke up every few hours she could get more warm milk down him. Without a doubt she saved the little goat's life, and I hated to tell her that her heroics were pointless. As gently as possible I tried to explain the gender specific facts of goat life.

Goats must be bred each year to keep them in milk. The offspring can either become future stock for milking or, if they are unfortunate enough to be born male, they often end up on someone's plate. I have never been willing to face the job of butchering a goat and so I always "pass the buck" to the many willing Hispanic families in the area for whom fresh goat meat—*chivo*—is a real delicacy.

One summer a doomed goat went to my own crew. My kitchen became the scene of an all-day multicultural culinary explosion as huge pots simmered with meat, beans, and thick mole sauce. Salads were prepared, stacks of tortillas made by hand, and sweet corn steamed and piled high. That evening we feasted, danced, and told stories around the fire pit at the base of the avocado orchard. I fully intended to eat some of the goat meat but ended up seated next to the lucky guest who got the head. I ate tortillas, beans, and sweet corn.

Although I have practiced vegetarianism on and off for most of my adult life, I remain ambivalent about raising animals for food. In part, these feelings were influenced by seeing the respectful and responsible way some indigenous cultures raise and kill animals. My travels also convinced me without a shadow of a doubt that industrial-style feedlots are no place for animals to live and no place for anyone's food to come from.

There is a strange paradox in this for those who think that by eating organic vegetables they are absolved of involvement with these deplorable places. Many organic farmers rely heavily on blood meal, bonemeal, and purchased composts to augment their soil fertility program. These fertilizers are the by-products of the worst of the livestock industry. The manures originate from feedlots where animals are jammed together in squalor, the blood and bonemeal from mass production slaughterhouses.

I am not blameless in this; I sometimes use blood meal on crops that consumers expect to be large in size. This is only one of the many compromises I face every day, when I drive my diesel-driven tractor, irrigate the California desert to grow lettuce, or load a male goat I have raised into a truck to meet his fate.

The domestic creatures on this farm—the chickens, goats, horse, and humans—live together in an imperfect, mutually dependent dance. We are all a little bit out of place in our neighborhood of tract homes and freeways, yet we are not part of the wild world either. From the kitchen window I can see the goats and the horse walking about in captivity. I do not like zoos, yet here I am the chief zookeeper.

I doubt that my goats discuss issues of freedom versus captivity while they lounge about in the dust of their pen. I think that what animals want most of all is peace of mind, a sense of being physically comfortable and safe from immediate danger, and to be part of a routine that allows them to live within their instincts. Perhaps it is presumptuous of me to think that I know what animals want. Maybe they look at me with my internal dilemmas and see me as the one who is in captivity, always questioning, trying to seek balance between the natural world and the one we have made tame.

Luis Goena came for Mars the goat on the appointed day and tied him into the big slat-sided truck. Luis keeps goats himself and so knows this sad routine well. But this time Fate had something else in mind. The Los Padres National Forest Service was looking for a few good goats to clear brush in the dry, fire-vulnerable hills above the Goleta Valley. Mars would be eating chaparral for a living.

5.

Perseverance

The sheriffs pulled up in front of my tractor, blocking my escape from the orchard. It was ten o'clock and so dark I couldn't see for sure, but it appeared that the two officers had their hands on their guns as they walked toward me. Their approach made it seem like I had committed some terrible crime.

I had. I had just carried out mass murder. Thousands of greenhouse thrips were now dying from the plant-derived sabadilla I had just sprayed. They deserved it. They were sucking the chlorophyll from the skins of the avocado crop, turning the fruit brown.

The cops were not that interested in insect problems, in the life cycle of this tiny pest, in the fact that the spray was botanical and relatively safe, or in the reasons why I was out with the tractor in the middle of the night. They just wanted me to stop making noise.

I was a little surprised at their indifference to the subtleties of pest control. For most people it is the first thing they ask when they learn I am an organic farmer.

I usually reply that we don't have many pests. The analogy is that if people eat well, sleep, and take care of their bodies, they usually don't get sick. It's the same with plants. When they are properly nurtured, grown from good seed, planted at the right time, and given proper moisture and well-balanced, healthy soil, they are rarely susceptible to insects or disease. There are exceptions.

The avocados were healthy and well cared for, yet the orchard was overpopulated with greenhouse thrips. I have since discovered an easy solution, one that does not attract the sheriff. My weapon is the most beautiful and ethereal of insects, the lacewing. It has a big appetite for thrips and, released into the orchard in sufficient numbers, protects the avocados.

I know all this now, but the first time I saw the thrip damage I felt like I had to *do* something. Spraying gave me a sense of power and control. I didn't realize that while I was spraying the pests, I was also spraying an invisible universe teeming with life.

There is a collision of worlds on this small farm. Humans, crops, and domestic animals are thrown together with predators, insects, and soil microbes, all operating in an enormous, interdependent matrix. It's like I'm always trying to merge in traffic, to make my goals and priorities slip into the stream of life that is balancing itself constantly in my fields.

It is tempting to manipulate the environment into straight rows and single species, to try to create a convenient system to suit the needs of our business. Within the larger natural system of the farm, however, I am just one participant among millions of forms of life who cross paths, are born, die, eat crops, eat each other, and decompose into the ground. My influence in that world is limited. Only by observation and experience can I gently tip the balance in favor of my crops. When farming at my best, I scarcely intervene at all.

This is not to say that pest disasters don't happen. It's just that by paying attention I have some time to react. Occasionally the invasion is instant and dramatic and comes as a complete surprise.

One Friday evening, I stopped to admire the large shiny leaves and stout plants of the strawberry planting just below the house. Laden with fruit at every stage from small and green to large and red and ready to pick, the plants looked beautiful. I looked down the rows, absorbing the satisfaction that comes from seeing full rows of healthy plants with no empty spaces. Then I finished loading the truck and left for the weekend to go camping with my son, knowing that the main spring cash crop was secure.

On Monday while unpacking the truck I caught a glimpse of the strawberry planting out of the corner of my eye. Something was not right. I walked down the hill to get a closer look and was shocked to discover that the leaves on most of the plants were brown and dry. Much of the fruit had begun to shrivel. It looked like someone had taken a torch to the entire field. The weather could not have gotten that hot, and the plants were well watered, so I looked closer. Barely visible on the underside of the leaves were tiny spider mites surrounded by a light webbing.

Shock turned to resolve. Out came the soap sprays to try to do in the mites; seaweed concentrate provided the dying plants with a nutrient boost. Our local entomologist came out with bottles of beneficial persimilis mites to release. We walked down the rows sprinkling these nearly invisible critters mixed with light soil onto the plants. Three weeks later the planting had almost recovered. New leaves emerged, hiding the dry brown ones, the plants were flowering again, and the rows were swarming with entomologists taking notes. They had never seen such a dramatic turnaround. "A miracle," they said.

In three and a half weeks this planting had gone from peak health to near death to almost complete recovery. I felt like I had just presided over a medical emergency triage and the victims had survived. I had managed to get the right bugs on my side.

Fairview Gardens is just loaded with bugs. Depending on your perspective you might say that some are "good," and some "bad." Oriental fruit moths, aphids, slugs and snails, cabbage loopers, thrips of every kind, cucumber, flea, and asparagus beetles, cutworms, spider mites, scales, lygus, and mealy bugs are all checked and balanced by mealy bug destroyers, lacewings, ladybugs, tachnid flies, trichogramma wasps, assassin bugs, hover flies, spined soldier bugs, and tiny pirate bugs. Most of them have their place in the ecology of the farm, but there are times when we need to interfere. The trick is knowing when.

Move slowly, I continually remind myself when I notice the first munchings on a leaf or fruit. Is this really worth reacting to? Has the infestation reached that economic threshold where the damage will be signifi-

80

cant? Or will more harm come to the ecological balance of the farm by interfering to save a few heads of cabbage or peaches or plums? Undisturbed meadows and native forests are rarely overrun by pests and diseases. Surely we can emulate these natural systems in the fields and

orchards by providing the proper conditions for plant health.

The idea was to learn to farm in nature's image, to make the farm into a self-contained ecosystem where ultimately no products from outside the system would be needed. At the same time, there seemed to be more instant, problem-solving products available by the day. Chemical companies seized on the emerging popularity of organic pesticides and fertilizers and began to market them with the same enthusiasm they bring to selling parathion, one of the deadliest poisons still legal in this country.

The onslaught of advertising and promotion is now so great that sometimes I actually feel I'm missing out or not doing a good job if I don't buy products. An arsenal of botanical poisons—sabadilla, neem, pyrethrin, quassia, ryania, rotenone, and nicotine are sold under catchy product names including Avid, Affirm, Neemisis, Drax, Perma Guard, Veratran D, Ryan 50, and Blackleaf 40.

All these products are available and legal for the new organic grower. They are far less toxic than parathion but come from the same mentality of solving problems with a miracle cure rather than by addressing the source of the problem. Though botanical and biological sprays are mostly safe for humans, they are still poisons, and don't just effect the targeted insect pest. In moments of desperation, when I fill my fiberglass spray

81

tank and start the engine and pump turning, I can't help but think of our beneficial insect friends who will unfortunately be affected by this heavy-handed solution. Rumbling down the rows, vibrating from tractor and sprayer, I put myself into the body and consciousness of the beneficial aphid midge or tiny hover fly. Picturing the frequencies at which the insect world operates, I imagine three hundred pounds per square inch of concentrated fluid barreling towards me, a tiny, weightless creature hanging onto a leaf, wildly blowing about from the force of the pressure. What's in that rumbling tank can make a thrip, or a worm, or an aphid really sick. If you are that small it will ruin your day.

Spraying is the worst way to solve an insect problem and is usually a last resort. Insect "problems" are generally a sign that something more fundamental is lacking in the system. If there is enough of an infestation to require plant-derived or biological insecticides, the real answer probably lies deeper. Was the crop planted at the wrong time or in too large a planting? Was it too wet or too dry? Is the soil lacking in fertility? Is the balance between beneficial and predatory insects out of whack?

For example, for several years a large percentage of our peach crop was misshapen and deformed due to lygus bugs. The tiny insects were sucking the juices out of the fruit. To combat them, I researched and experimented with every possible organic spray. Nothing worked. As it turned out, we were actually part of the problem: the lygus were living in the cover crop we planted in the alleys between the trees. Each spring, when the fruit was small and vulnerable, we mowed that cover crop and turned it in, displacing the insects and forcing them into the closest lush green environment, in this case the peach trees. Simply waiting to mow the cover crop until the fruit was developed and leaving habitat for the lygus corrected this so-called pest problem.

As I rammed about over the years madly planting everything I could think of, as the medley of crops increased, pest problems decreased. Unconsciously, I had done the best thing possible to preserve balance. Soon the crew and I learned to do it on purpose, rotating crops in an

On Timing and Weeds

Good farmers know that timing is everything. Constant observation and anticipation and proactivity versus reactivity, make the difference between failure and success. Planting when the soil moisture is correct, at the right phase of the moon, at the right time of year for the crop or variety, even the right time of the day can lead to dramatic differences in germination, plant vigor, and pest resistance. When dealing with "weeds," timing is especially critical. Remember that "weeds" are merely plants out of place and that weed competition is primarily a problem in the early stages of crop development.

Three things resolve weed competition easily: early cultivation, the right tool, and attitude. The goal is to never weed but to cultivate. Cultivation aerates the soil around the plants, and cuts off or buries young tender weeds. If you have to actually weed, you are too late and will have created far more work for yourself.

ever-changing crazy quilt, creating an agricultural ecosystem that eventually integrated into the natural one.

At certain times of the year, above the sound of traffic, sirens, and airplanes overhead, the farm symphony affirms this as calls of birds, crickets, and frogs blend with the crowing, neighing, and bleating of the domestic animals. The sounds reassure me that such diversity exists, that the hidden life on the farm is alive and busy, pollinating, feeding, and protecting crops. Frogs and toads feed on slugs and cutworms, chickens on flies and snails, birds eat worms and aphids, and armies of predatory insects maintain order in the fields and orchards.

In a way there really are no pests on the farm, only imbalances caused by our misperceptions. Once, in a French film made with special cameras and insect-eye-view lenses, I saw the most beautifully sensual footage of two snails mating. It was conscious love in action, or so it seemed. As I watched I couldn't help but remember that most of my adult life I have smashed, trapped, collected, and otherwise battled snails. For good reason. They have enormous appetites and do not merely nibble. A morning discovery on young tender plants is often a discovery too late. Seeing them in that film gave me a new sense of respect. Almost enough respect to stop killing them.

Drought. Six o'clock in the morning and already the sun was hot. Coyotes wandered down the middle of Fairview Avenue, the deer braved suburban traffic in search of food, birds ate our seedlings, and bees congregated around a dripping faucet.

Several years without substantial rain had left the native grasses and plants in the hills above the farm bone dry. Wild animals traveled into the city seeking green. Even in the city, lawns and golf courses were left to turn brown. Water was carefully allotted; a green lawn became a crime.

The farm had been given a rationed water allotment, one based on historic use. In this system, those farmers who over the years had been

carelessly sloshing water around were rewarded with higher allotments; those of us who had been conserving paid for our careful ways. Forced to experiment, we discovered that careful cultivation conserved moisture. Deeper planting depths, mulches, and drip irrigation systems helped stretch every droplet. Smaller fruit, with sweeter and more intense flavor, often resulted. Some customers complained about fruit size and higher costs. They saw it larger and cheaper from Spain or Israel, at the local supermarket.

It was hard not to worry about a future without rain. I pondered what we would grow, trying not to think about what we would have to give up. Avocados, sweet corn, and lettuces would give way to dry beans, carob, and olives. I couldn't imagine how this community, with its twenty-four-hour access to anything from anywhere, would take to a diet of tepary beans, dry corn, or carob.

My worry increased as huge old specimen trees began dying from thirst; our tall pines that define the center of the land were stressed. We watched over our water meter like crazed investors, knowing that exceeding the imposed limit would be too expensive to bear. I, who came to California seeking the sun and refuge from the gray and cloudy, would wake up and curse another clear and brilliant day.

At the peak of the drought I flew from Santa Barbara to the place where I grew up in Delaware. On takeoff I marveled at the dry, moonlike landscape below me. Six hours later, I was driving toward my father's home through lush green on both sides of the road. There was a light rain. I was hypnotized by the drops on the windshield and the back and forth swish that took them away.

This was the home that I left as a teenager to go west. At sixteen, I wanted to get as far as possible from the industrial east and break free of the small-town state of Delaware. Now my eyes feasted on deep green grasses, lush foliage of maples and beech, and drops of liquid life falling from the sky. The air felt cool and alive and I wondered why I ever left.

My father tempted me (as he always does) with a piece of land that

Water Wisdom

Water with care. Water is precious. Recent wars have been fought over oil; in the future they may be fought over water. Build the organic matter in your soil and your land will become like a sponge. Mulch, then mulch some more. Water deeply and less frequently; most plants prefer less water to too much. Find out what food crops really belong in your climate and experiment with them. Use drip tapes, micro sprinklers, soaker hose, and automatic time clocks to help conserve. Most importantly, use and develop your sensitivity to what is happening in the soil, what the plant is telling you, and when to wait and when to water.

When growing food, water for tenderness and flavor, not just to keep plants alive. When growing tomatoes we irrigate only to get the plants to a certain height (sometimes only three to four waterings) and then stop. While fruit size can suffer slightly, the improved flavor and sugars in the fruit make it a worthwhile practice. Crops like lettuces and greens want to be moist all of the time. Experiment and adjust the frequency and amount of irrigation for each crop.

has stayed within my family. For a moment I considered moving back, thinking how much extra time I could have if I didn't have to irrigate. I began to plan what I could do with winters off and longed for green instead of desperate brown.

My thoughts of moving were intensified by my recent divorce. The farm and the orchards that Donna and I nurtured and the house where we raised our son together seemed to have lost their energy in the complexities and pain of our split. But leaving Fairview Gardens permanently was not the answer.

This was not the first time I had traveled away from the farm or considered leaving altogether. Often, when the suburban development would close in on me in a type of modern agricultural claustrophobia, or when the phone calls, visitors, and paperwork got to me, I would leave—sometimes, if it were winter, for months at a time. This travel gave me perspective and an extraordinary chance to see what other farmers were thinking and doing. Though I didn't realize it, all this travel would also open up the path to Fairview's future, which at the time of my first big trip seemed non-existent, doomed by drought.

In 1986, in the first year of the drought, I spent three months in China to see firsthand the oldest agricultural tradition in the world. For the first time I saw fertile land that had been farmed over and over, not for decades as in the United States, but for thousands of years. This intensive style of farming, on raised beds with crops intermingled and waste recycled, introduced me to a kind of resource management that made my efforts at sustainable farming seem like the strugglings of a beginner.

Each time I traveled, I returned to find Fairview still healthy, thanks to the efforts of Salvador Gomez, Steve Soderquist, and the crew. I would join in again, full of new ideas. At times I think Salvador, who comes from an old farming family in Mexico, must have been amused by all of it.

Over the course of ten years, I traveled nearly every winter. In the Peruvian Andes I saw people adapting their agriculture to land so steep that farmers had been known to fall out of their fields. In Sicily and

Hopiland, cultures survive on harsh land through their intimate connection to the earth and each other. In the mountains of Burundi, in Africa, farmers live alongside their fields, these fields ringing their homes in concentric circles of crops and pastureland.

Food and water were not taken for granted in these places. Food and life were not separate. The ecological sensitivity of these farmers was not intellectually derived but born out of the need to eat and to insure that soil and farmland survived. Unlike American farmers, they could not abandon spent land and move on to the next irrigated valley.

Organic as practiced in most traditional agriculture was not some quaint idea nor was it predicated on the demands of consumers for safe food. In some cases pesticides, herbicides, and commercial fertilizers were just too costly, and regenerating the soil and encouraging a healthy ecosystem on the land was simply practical for future survival. It insured both sustainable production and food for the next generation.

What started as an opportunity to get away and gain perspective on my own life and farming soon became an obsession. I began writing and photographing to create a visual diary of my travels and experiences. I also visited America's desolate industrial farms, and saw innovative, smaller scale farms all over the United States and Europe where farming and community were linked in new, modern ways. The line between my work on the farm and my observations in other parts of the world began to blur, and the accumulated materials from the travels began to affect my daily life.

In February of 1991, I attended a meeting with local farmers at the Goleta library. Those gathered were desperate; we were at the end of what normally was our rainy season without a drop. On the table was an emergency measure to alleviate the crisis. It involved towing fresh-water icebergs down from Alaska and parking them off the coast of Goleta where they could melt and supply the local thirsty farms. This was a serious proposal.

Miracle March started on March 17 at about two o'clock in the afternoon. I had just opened up some new ground on the slope of the front field when the sky let loose like somebody had opened a huge valve. It poured. Within one hour we had three inches, and Salvador and I were scrambling to keep our newly disced soil in place. Gullies were forming and we worked frantically to dig diversion ditches to carry off the excess water. The rains were coming faster than the ground could absorb.

Miracle March restored the water resources in a few weeks of rain. But the experiences of the drought and my travels stayed with me, reflected in my changing perspective on Fairview's role in the community.

6.

Corn Earworms and Melons in March

At 4:31a.m., the old farmhouse started to roll like a ship, pitching me out of bed. I grabbed Aaron and headed out the back door in time to see the electricity go off in a wave down the coast, to be replaced by an array of brilliant, and usually invisible, stars.

When the sun came out that morning, it was one of those perfectly still, crystal clear days that often follow an earthquake. I thought I should go investigate to see if the world around me still existed. What better way to feel the pulse of our suburban neighborhood than to visit the local supermarket? So I walked the few blocks to the shopping center. Cars collided in midintersection (the traffic lights were still out) and lines formed at the gas station as people waited for the electric pumps to come back on. When I stepped inside the door of Vons on this brilliant, sunny day it was completely dark. Ice cream melted in the freezers, meat spoiled in the deli, and hordes of people frantically filled their carts using flashlights to navigate the aisles. In the frenzy, it struck me how fragile and precarious our food system really is.

Fairview Gardens' first produce stand was made of four four-by-eight-foot wooden panels—the remains of an old chicken coop. Ron Luikhart and I dragged the panels down to the northeast corner of the farm, stood them on their sides, nailed the corners together, and created a roof for shade out of some old plywood. We made signs for the road, planted six three-hundred-foot rows of large bloom zinnias leading up to our new store, and began planting sweet corn in the front field in two-week successions.

The structure didn't have a door so we had to climb in over the counter. My neighbor James put on the stereotype overalls and straw hat and became the first salesperson. I refused to sacrifice valuable field space for parking, so there was just enough space between the field and the stand for people to drive up to the counter and roll down their windows for service. Inevitably someone would pull up and give their order like at the fast food drive-up: "Gimme two tomatoes, a couple peaches, a head of romaine, and an ear of corn and hold the worms." James handed it over and they'd spin out of the driveway, sending a cloud of dust over everything.

One night someone drove off the road drunk and crashed into the stand. He did us a big favor. We had outgrown our chicken coop-turned-sales-shack, and it surely would have fallen down if someone had not run into it. The demolition also gave us a chance to build something we had always talked about, a structure that was not just a sales outlet but provided roadside audience-participation theater. Using two-by-fours and plywood, we built a kind of shaded amphitheater, thirty feet wide at the front and tapering towards the back. When people parted the garlic braids lining the entrance like beads in the Casbah, it was as if they emerged into a giant, living cornucopia of fruit, flowers, and vegetables.

The new stand shattered every zoning law and architectural rule of design. We topped off our concept of open-air food theater with a huge blue and white striped awning that rolled up and down over the entire front of the building. Each day, when we opened the stand, it was like lifting the curtain for the show to begin. The main attraction was fresh picked sweet corn and we added to the performance by parading by with bags of corn from the fields flourishing a few feet away.

95

At the produce stand in summer, the corn earworm rules. Plump and corn-colored with dark stripes and a dark head it nestles into the end of the ears, hidden by the silky husks, nibbling daintily. It only stops eating long enough to look up with disdain at a lady in high heels as she makes her way through twelve ears, tearing each open to find the perfect one. There's something primal about the meeting of woman and beast, especially when they are after the same piece of food.

When we first started selling corn, people would scream and throw down the corn when they encountered an earworm. Now there is always one customer in the crowd around the corn bin who calms the fears of the rest, explaining that the worms are a sign that no poisons were used. There are now customers who believe that the only ear worth eating is one that has been kissed by a worm.

Corn anchors the summer and fall seasons at the produce stand; in spring customers come looking for strawberries, and things become more complicated.

One afternoon in May, a brand new Volvo station wagon still bearing the dealer's plates pulled in and parked. A father with three young children in tow walked into the stand. Upon discovering that the price of our berries was about thirty-five cents more than at the local supermarket, Dad wheeled around and dragged his three now screaming kids out the door. I wished I had the opportunity to explain what that extra thirty-five cents was buying.

Strawberries are the most chemically intensive crop in California and receive some 300 pounds of chemicals per acre each year. They are difficult to grow organically. Commercial growers turn to a dangerous, ozone-depleting chemical, methyl bromide, to kill weeds and pathogens and to sterilize the soil in which the plants grow. For the remaining nine months of their lives, the berry plants are fed chemical fertilizers to substitute for the fertility that was lost to methyl bromide, like patients on an intravenous drip.

It has taken us years of experimentation to devise a truly viable organic alternative. Our method is labor intensive and more expensive to execute, but it does not involve methyl bromide or a single one of the sixty-five pesticides registered for use on strawberries.

Had the father in the Volvo known this, he might have considered Fairview's berries to be at least as good a value as his airbags and antilock brakes. And that's before he tasted them.

In February or March, people rush in breathless, bundled in down jackets or carrying umbrellas, asking for melons or tomatoes for a dinner party. We patiently explain that we only carry what we grow ourselves, that melons, corn, and tomatoes are heat-loving plants that grow only in summer, and that in winter there are a number of wonderful foods being harvested: spinach, lettuce, mandarin oranges, asparagus, leeks, and sugar snap peas.

When we first started selling food direct to this community we never used the word "organic." Organic then was considered a bit weird, practiced by longhaired people with bare feet, who weren't sophisticated enough to get the techno-chemical thing straight. Instead we tried to focus on taste and freshness. Give someone a tree ripe peach or a strawberry picked hours before and nothing need be said. People eventually wanted to know more. How was this grown? What materials were used to grow it? When was it harvested?

In 1991 my partner, now wife, Jeanne-Marie Herman moved onto the farm and took over the management of the stand. I met Jeanne-Marie in 1986 at the local farmers' market. Our friendship developed over many meals and across many countries as she accompanied me on some of my photographic journeys. When she came to live on the farm, we held the romantic notion of working together on the land. She transformed the stand into a bustling store and filled the nooks and corners of the farm with flower gardens.

It was not as romantic as we planned. Most of our evenings were

Simple Pleasures

Instead of going out to the movies or straining to see your friends or family across a linen-covered candlelit table, passively waiting to be fed, hoping that the chef is in a good mood, and the ingredients were harvested within the last century, try staying home. Spend a slow afternoon or evening with those same friends and family planning, harvesting, collecting, preparing, and eating a meal together. Go grazing if you grow your own, and allow the meal to create itself as you wander through garden or fields. Wash, chop, and cook together to some music. Finally settle in to a long, deliberate, slow, passionate meal. Experience love made manifest through food.

spent talking shop, and the realities of working and living in Grand Central Station were trying. Jeanne-Marie wanted a more peaceful life, with dried flowers hanging in the windows, leisurely evening walks on the land, and most of all, a quiet and private home. There was nothing quiet or private about this farm; it was a circus.

Meanwhile the produce stand was becoming the modern version of the neighborhood mom and pop store (except that mom and pop were trying to work it out). Young, eager employees arrived ready to commit for life until a friend planned a surf trip. Equally energetic replacements always appeared. Some stayed for a summer, others worked their way through college. The customers are more regular. Ben and Rose pulled in every day from the New Horizons retirement community to pick up their daily fix of tomatoes and corn and stayed to chat. For years, Julia and David came every Friday to load the trunk of their Mercury Cougar with boxes of produce for the cancer patients they cared for.

Kids barely out of the car run up to the animals, clutching one of the carrots or bruised apples we keep behind the counter. Sometimes, our feeble intercom system works as a communications tool between the produce stand and the house, and orders for "more corn" or beans or berries or basil come squawking through. Then it's off on the bicycle stationed outside the door for the downhill, high-speed race to the fields. Sometimes if we run out of eggs, customers wander off to collect for themselves. Occasionally an overeager egg collector will be discovered trapped inside the chicken coop, having entered through the tiny ramp built for the chickens. Or a well-intentioned customer will go off excitedly for basil only to return with a bunch of malva in hand.

Our first order for green tomatoes came from a southern gentleman who had just moved to the area. We always prided ourselves on harvesting dead ripe and I was a bit taken aback by this request. I agreed on the basis that he would bring us a sample, breaded and fried. Similar bargains were struck with other customers and soon zucchini or kabocha squash started returning to us in breads or pies. Recipes flew back and forth as our weekly newsletter (*All the News that's Fit to Eat*) revealed the closely guarded secrets of Three Blender Pesto, Ableman's Famous Gazpacho, and Hong Kong Fuey's Wok and Woll.

On a typical Wednesday morning in midsummer, I was trying to fit 10 boxes of corn, 28 boxes of tomatoes, 150 bunches of basil, 85 bags of salad mix, 16 cartons of sweet peppers, 12 flats of cherry tomatoes, 8 boxes of eggplant, 7 cases of 'Ambrosia' cantaloupe, and 5 boxes of French beans onto a rusty 1981 half-ton Toyota truck.

By the time I completed this predawn puzzle, the truck was stacked eight feet above the bed, tables and umbrellas balancing on top. Tying it all down was the ultimate challenge—too tight and I risked crushing the products, too loose and the hundred-mile stretch

of highway between Santa Barbara and the Santa Monica farmers' market would be sprinkled with a colorful array of summer vegetables.

103

The little blue truck hated Wednesdays and responded like a burro being loaded for a long trek. With each added box the suspension groaned. Each time I put my body into the rope and pulled, the truck leaned to one side. In seven years of doing that trip, I only lost eight boxes of peaches, one antique scale, and three watermelons. My helper and I couldn't abandon the juicy broken melons. Even though we were late for market, we had to stop and eat them sitting by the side of the road.

As hard as we tried and as early as we got started, we always seemed to arrive at the market moments before they closed the street. About one hundred growers already lined the streets, standing next to their flatbed trucks or new Isuzu Bobtails waiting to begin setting up. We inched our way through the streets like the last float in a parade, the rusty blue toy truck top heavy and swaying from side to side. I eventually replaced the truck with a newer white one, making for a less conspicuous entrance.

The market ritual seldom varies. Once in our spot we jockey for position. Each grower is assigned a space but the early birds squeeze the latecomers a bit, setting the stage for what I refer to as the "space wars." Order is restored as the market manager patrols with her tape measure moving people one foot in one direction, two in the other. When the street officially closes to traffic we race to create an entire sales outlet in the hour before the market opens. Tables and awnings go up and displays are constructed. "Pass me the beans, I'll pile them in the center. Tomatoes over here, five boxes in width. Should we do 'em at a dollar a pound? Salad goes under the umbrella, let's alternate the peppers yellow, red, orange, chocolate, and red again. Don't forget to keep the Habaneros out of reach of the children!"

Crowds gather—"We can't sell until the bell is rung," we tell the same man every week when he comes early hoping to avoid the crowds. While they wait to buy our food they pelt us with questions "How much is this?" "Fifty cents?" The same lady always cuts the price in half. "Is it sweet?" "Put this one aside for me, will ya?" Basil is strewn everywhere, the last few items are put up, the truck checked, and all the extra boxes

How to Sell Garlic, Basil, and Tomatoes

These three good friends not only go well together in fields and in the pot, they provide a fragrant and visually seductive display when placed together at the market. Garlic is easily sold by smashing several cloves throughout the day on the pavement in front of your stand. As the day wears on and the pavement heats up, the aroma draws crowds in to buy. Tomatoes must be piled in huge heaps with the stem end down, with several sliced open on top of the stack and a knife always at the ready to slice open a fresh sample. If there are several varieties, alternate shapes and colors. Cherry tomatoes are attractive displayed in baskets in a checkerboard pattern with alternating colors, yellow and red. Basil should be draped all around the tomato display, used as dividers for the different varieties, and placed so the bunches are constantly in the way. When you have a crowd, take a bouquet of basil and, waving it gently, move down the line from nose to nose, providing a brief aromatic experience. Every person who smells will surely buy.

stacked within easy reach. When the bell rings we are frantic as customers pack in three deep across the length of our tables.

If we are the only grower with red peppers or Japanese eggplants or French beans, within moments the word is out and we are mobbed. Twelve full bags hang suspended from outstretched arms, customers crowd forward, some shaking the bags up and down demanding that they be the next. A woman hands me a bag with two peaches and when I turn my back to weigh them proceeds to steal ten more. My market partner yells, then chases the thief through the crowds. Most of the time we carry on like we are on stage, guessing weights before the bags hit the scale, threatening to dive into the heap of green beans, and juggling cantaloupes. Occasionally the market managers reprimand us for our shenanigans or for the continuous flow of samples we provide to every passerby.

Sometimes at these markets it feels like the growers and the fresh food are the last lingering connection to the natural world. Women linger to chat, asking us questions like we are exotic creatures from the land. A woman with a pendulum tests the vibrations of our food before buying. A young producer-type stops to buy French beans while negotiating a long distance deal on his cell phone. The beans are $1.50, his deal probably in the millions.

Men with pinstriped suits and manicured fingernails ask us to select their food for them. Perhaps they are afraid of getting dirty. We hand out slices of melon or cherry tomatoes. In an instant, the shoppers are children again, giggling as juice runs down their faces and new flavors transport them to another time and place. For this moment urban and rural, earth and concrete blend and meld together.

Winter night, 1991. Ten-fifteen and the sky was clear, no wind, zero air movement, the temperature plummeting. The farm thermometer was broken so I drove down the street to check the reading on the digital billboard in front of the local bank. It was already thirty-four degrees and the electronic device dropped one more degree in the moments I cruised past. At home the weather radio confirmed heavy inversion frost warnings in low-lying areas. I remembered the consequences of the last big freeze years earlier.

I had no special equipment and no practical way to protect the orchard. To the north, growers were renting helicopters to hover over orchards to draw down warmer air. Smudge pots filled with diesel spewed an acrid black smoke offering a few degrees of relief, and wind machines roared in local canyons. It was futile. The temperature was headed below the damage point of twenty-eight degrees and I knew that nothing would help with this type of freeze.

The next morning the avocado and cherimoya orchards were dying branch by branch. First the leaves turned a sickly black, then the smaller branches; eventually some trees gave in completely. The orchards looked like that for a month. We could not begin to prune until we gave the trees enough time to show what was actually dead and what might recover.

We had always relied too heavily on avocados. It's very tempting as they are as close to money trees as any crop can be. There are few places in the country where they grow well, and our location at the north end of California's production zone brings us consistently higher late-season prices and much needed fall income. Avocados require no pruning and have few problems from invading pests. Their main enemy is a freeze.

A state of disaster was declared for a number of agricultural areas in California and for the first time we went on the agricultural dole. It would be two years before the surviving trees would be back in production. Fairview's economic survival was on the line. We applied for and received a meager check to cover the costs of orchard rehabilitation and a fraction of the loss. I felt guilty receiving those funds, but reminded myself of the $46 million per day in subsidies that flows from taxpayers' pockets to large scale industrial farms.

A fellow grower responded to his freeze devastation by adopting a distribution model I had seen during my travels called Community

Supported Agriculture (CSA). The name makes it sound like some sort of welfare program for small farms, but the idea is actually one of mutual support. It's a return to a form of social agriculture where community members take a share of the farmer's risk in exchange for a share of the harvest. They do this by paying up front for a weekly portion of the fruit and vegetable harvest, thereby becoming members of the CSA. In this way the farm has capital to begin the year. In some CSAs the members participate in the workings of the farm, helping to plan the season's planting, and even joining in the work in the fields if they choose. We started our own CSA the following year with forty families.

Now, Thursday mornings are a scramble. We've got 125 families to feed and the food has to be harvested by noon. The crew picks the lettuce first, then other leafy greens, then carrots and beets, turnips and radish if we have them, potatoes and berries, leeks and lemons, avocados, asparagus and on and on. At midday we set up the tables under a shade area built next to the produce stand and begin putting out food so fresh that it almost jumps out of the boxes onto the table.

At one-thirty folks start rolling in with baskets, buckets, large bags, and boxes of every shape, size, and material. They check off their names, pick up a newsletter and begin the mouth-watering journey down the tables, following the list and amounts recommended on the board. A trade table is set up so members who just can't get into kale or turnips can leave these behind and pick up the carrots or beets that someone else has left. There is a hum of activity as families visit the animals, discuss recipes, and load up their food.

I am nagged by the question of how to go beyond the world of commerce, to take this idea of total nourishment further. The concept of the CSA model is sound, but the gulf between idea and practice is still too wide. The CSA, which is supposed to give families a chance to be on the land and closer to the source of their food, is stuck in the realm of economics. People like the idea because they feel it is a good value. Even then, many have become accustomed to the unlimited choice that supermarkets offer. Some struggle with the fact that the weekly share of food is only what that season provides, no cucumbers in December, corn in January, or melons in March.

With busy lives to live, our members' participation often begins and ends with the payment at the beginning of the season and the box of food received each week. We have worked together to change this by offering potlucks, tours, and other opportunities to get involved. But the world seems to be moving a little too fast for that. Food and farms, like everything else, must be convenient.

Ann Wisehart and her husband Mike Glick live in a suburban tract home and were employed in defense research and design when they first discovered the farm. Now their front and back lawn has been replaced with corn, berries, tomatoes, and fruit trees. They paid off their mortgage, quit their jobs and have become examples of the grow-your-own lifestyle. I like to think that our food had something to do with these life changes, that being involved with the farm changed the way they thought about other things as well.

I see less of Ann and Mike these days, not because they don't like me or the farm, they just don't need me anymore. Their own garden is full. They have observed our techniques, borrowed seeds and ideas, and created a suburban homestead. A couple of months ago they asked me to come over and help graft one of their fruit trees. This time they served me food from their garden (dinners used to be from my own) and we grafted Satsuma plum by the light of a flashlight.

Last week they came to the farm for a birthday party with a peach pie handmade from their own peaches. I have always preached that I look forward to the day when families and individuals put farmers out of business by growing their own. Now I worry. Planting a few vegetables in the front or back yard is one thing, but that home grown peach pie is another matter.

7.

Fertile Minds

For five days in the spring of 1989, twenty-five third graders took over the farm. The kids were divided into groups: the Carrots, the Goats, the Cucumbers, the Spades, and the Hoes. They rotated through a variety of jobs: milking, baking bread, harvesting, preparing meals, making compost, feeding animals, hoeing weeds, and working at the produce stand. Their teacher and I, plus various parents, were on hand to help manage the chaos.

We used an air horn to call them together for meals and twenty-five little bodies scrambled out of every nook and cranny on the farm. At night we had fire circles with music, arrowhead making, wreath making, and story telling.

The first night there were a number of cries of "I wanna go home." By the end of the second day, home was a distant memory replaced by thoughts of fresh strawberries, goats, and the wonders of earthworms and living soil. Parents were surprised to find that their kids were too occupied to acknowledge them. They were even more surprised to see their sons or daughters scarfing down fresh vegetables at mealtime.

The motto of the Waldorf school that these kids attended is "Teach the whole child: head, heart, and hands." Five days on the farm fulfilled those goals. I was exhausted at the end of the week, but pleased to see the kids leave with their clothes dirty, their faces stained with strawberry juice, and their hearts and minds filled with memories of the earth.

This was a rare educational experience for local kids and it wasn't long before the word spread. Other schools and groups called with requests. Not all of them came from such privileged backgrounds.

"Mr. Ableman, I got some money, would you take me to 7-11?" It was only the first few hours into a four-day live-in program and the 10-year-old boy tugging on my pants leg was insistent. I reminded him that during the next few days we'd only be eating food prepared from what was growing on the farm. We wouldn't be going to the local 7-11 convenience store.

The boy was with Rites of Passage, a group of fatherless boys from south central Los Angeles. Most of these boys had never seen a farm before, much less harvested and eaten fresh food from the ground. The first thing we did was go "grazing." I let them loose within the rows of the tall cherry tomato vines and watched their brain cells exploding with new information as they harvested and ate vine ripe tomatoes for the first time in their lives. We split open watermelons still warm from the sun and feasted on the hearts. This was real education—no plant identification exercises or in-depth lectures on soil, just the experience of seeing and eating food in context.

When I was a kid, creeks and fields lay within biking distance of my home. At my grandparents' cottage surrounded by open space, summers were filled with fresh food. I had my quiet places, my secret sanctuaries, and my make-believe world. Most city kids have nowhere to go to find elements of nature and the sense of place they provide.

At Fairview, kids find open space and hidden spots for their forts. They experience the smells and the feel of soft ground under their feet, play king of the mountain on the large compost piles and hide-and-go-seek amongst the maze and tangle of our peach and avocado orchards. This is a place where they can be free and feel connected to the earth. They can let go of the world of shopping malls and video games. For a little while, they can forget the intensity of peer pressures. Here it is OK to like fruits and vegetables. Though I discourage kids from picking foods without asking, I don't mind seeing the odd orange peel or carrot top left behind from a spontaneous snack.

I don't have any answers about the life the boys in Rites of Passage face everyday. I do know that after a few hours on the farm they reacted, as all kids do, to something instinctive. On the last day I gathered them together. I gave them each an avocado seed and told them how to germinate it—how to prepare a pot and some soil mix to plant it, and how to water and watch over it. They took those seeds as a continuation and memory of their experiences on the farm. It has been several years now and I dare to hope that in some neighborhood in the heart of south central Los Angeles a few avocado trees thrive and maybe even bear fruit.

Fairview's nursery manager Thomas Cole came to the farm as an intern after clearing land mines in Mozambique. Though it would be hard to find any work as intense and tedious as that, consider hand-seeding flats of lettuce or broccoli. Seed by single seed, each is placed into little individual cells, two hundred cells per tray, into hundreds of flats. This time-consuming and exacting ritual takes place each week in the small, shadehouse nursery we reclaimed from the blackberry brambles and snails. It is not hard to imagine why Tom has become the farm jester. Thanks to his antics, everyone watches their backs for fear of being hit with an overripe tomato, or soaked with an irrigation hose purposely aimed off course.

There are times when the future of our farm sits in that nursery waiting in thousands of little black plastic cells full of peat, sifted compost, and exploded volcanic rock. Eggplants, peppers, tomatoes, broccoli, and cabbage share a space the size of a single-car garage with endive, celery, raddichio, artichokes, and lettuce. Some twenty thousand tiny plants sprout in this protected space. The beginnings of any season are here in these black plastic trays.

We often start interns in the nursery, or in the small salad garden that grows directly in front of it. These are manageable jobs; jobs on a scale more easily understood than in the larger fields. Internships at Fairview Gardens, I caution each applicant, are not for everyone. To learn anything from the chaos of this small farm, interns must be patient and willing to dig in. We don't offer formal classes to interns. The classroom is the fields, and the learning comes from observing and doing, often for long, repetitive hours. Housing is rustic—a tent under the avocados or maybe a space in a trailer. The food is abundant, based on the time of the year and what is growing in the fields.

David Retsky was one intern I thought would never make it. He arrived from Beverly Hills at the age of twenty barely able to discern a carrot from a beet. After working for two years with us, he is now helping to run a farm on an East Coast college campus. Alexander Lejeune, who came to us from helping former gang members run a tortilla business in the heart of east Los Angeles, stayed to run our farmers' markets and CSA program. Former intern Heather Carney is now running a garden project at a school for developmentally disabled youth, Tara Angeletti runs a farm at a graduate institute, and other Fairview graduates work in agriculture throughout the country. In a time when the average age of an American farmer is sixty-two, such success is heartening.

Farming can be tedious and difficult work. Learning to farm takes patience. Given the demands of each day, there is no time to teach by explaining. Many lessons take a season or more to unfold. Most interns find that as time goes on they learn, one way or another, until they can look back and see that like the plants and trees, they too have grown.

When I first came to the farm I walked the land alone most of the time. Even as the crew and the produce stand expanded, and our duties grew to include trips to the farmers' market, the days were relatively quiet and focused on the job at hand. Now there are visitors around all of the time. They come from Japan, Korea, Singapore, Czechoslovakia, England, Ireland, Australia, Germany, France, and throughout the United States. They are agriculturists, entomologists, parents, teachers, doctors, spiritualists, healers, and sometimes just lovers of good food. Some arrive in tour buses with translators and take hours to understand our work. Others get out of their cars, look around, maybe buy a tomato or a peach, and drive on. Some linger with their children. My personal commitment is that each and every person who comes onto the farm come away inspired in some small way. I am not always able to live up to that commitment.

John Stewart called on his cellular phone to see if he could come "check out" the farm. He was here from Australia on holiday and never mentioned that anyone else was with him. I agreed to have him come by the next day, and told him I would say hello and then let him wander around. At the appointed time, two bus-loads of people arrived. I decided I had better take the time and give them a tour. I didn't find out until later that my guests were associated with huge industrial farms in Australia, and were determined practitioners of techno-chemical based farming.

It was late winter and to the untrained eye it appeared that the fields of cover crops were a tangled mess of weeds. About two sentences into my talk, a loud voice boomed from the back, "I have never seen such a bunch of trash in me life!"

In my insulated world I forget that not everyone views our work with pleasure; in fact some are threatened by what we represent. Change, or examples of change, can be difficult for those who are heavily invested in another way of doing things. I did end up giving that tour. Some, including the heckler, walked away and waited in the bus; the rest apologized for the outburst and joined our walk. And while we didn't necessarily agree with each other on approach, a healthy and respectful dialogue was initiated. I like to think that this experience may have opened up one or two minds about another way to farm.

In 1989, twelve hundred people converged on the farm for Farm Day Jamboree. Cops directed traffic out on Fairview Avenue, our "vegetable security team" in T-shirts with dancing vegetables watched over the fields, and the food and music flowed. Five hundred avocado-tomato sandwiches were assembled, baby artichokes were steamed, drums full of fresh lemonade were consumed, and the world's largest organic salad was offered from a kiddie pool.

It was our first annual event. The organizers scraped up funds by selling lemonade, advertised by distributing flyers, and fought over whether to offer organic hamburgers. This was real grassroots, evidenced by the diversity of farmers and organizations that came to participate or set up information booths. A kids' festival took place behind the house with apple bobbing, potato sack races, face painting, and tugs of war. A team of Belgian horses pulled wagons full of people through the tight roadways of the farm, and live bluegrass music from the farmhouse porch rolled out and into the fields and the neighborhood.

The following year Neil Woodall played his lively folk music to an audience of dancing five-to ten-year-olds, and in 1991 we had our first peach festival honoring the peak of our infamous harvest. We created a one-thousand-pound peach mountain, and The Acousticats fiddled for 500 dancing maniacs. We partied until Peach Mountain eroded away and the peach-colored light had faded from the sky.

In 1993, the community gathered on the farm to launch my first book *From the Good Earth*. The book brought surprising notoriety to the little farm as interviews aired and articles were printed from London and Sydney to New York and Los Angeles. I didn't realize at the time the impact all this attention would have. The media were fascinated with how this little farm had survived and flourished with the pressures of the surrounding development. I encouraged the attention hoping that our efforts might inspire others.

Fairview Gardens turned one hundred years old in 1995. One hundred years ago this valley boasted some of the richest topsoil on the West Coast, some thirty feet deep in places. Now shopping centers, gas stations, and fast food restaurants have replaced the family farms and ranches that once thrived here. At Fairview's centennial celebration I put forth the following question to an audience of eight hundred people: "What do we as a community want to see on this land for the next ten, twenty, fifty, or one hundred years?"

We can all survive without another condominium, Taco Bell, or shopping center. Can we really survive without fertile soils, without fresh and unpoisoned food, without a place to teach our children about interconnections and context, or a place to gather on the land?

Goleta Valley Junior High is only two blocks from the farm. It stands like a concrete block monolith and feels more like a minimum security prison than a place to open and expand the minds of seven hundred children.

I visited my son Aaron there for lunch one day. As I made my way through the throngs of screaming kids to the cafeteria, I expected to find students with trays in hand, lined up to be served a hot lunch by women in white aprons and hairnets. Instead the kitchen was shut down. The orderly lines had been abandoned for vending machines and students made a mad dash for Pizza Hut, Snapple, and microwave burritos. No wonder Aaron didn't want to bring a lunch. He reluctantly told

me that most days he would sneak off to the restroom to eat his sandwich of freshly harvested tomatoes, basil, and cucumber, embarrassed to be so different.

Now, when seventh graders assemble for a tour of the farm, some of them chew gum and look bored. Most are at least cautious about seeming too interested. Gathered on the knoll beneath the sycamore, I ask them to imagine that they are flying over the Goleta Valley, visualizing the sea of tract homes, their school, the street they walked to get here, and then this small oasis. I want them to think about where they are, about the context of this place. Eventually I bring them back down to the ground. We walk and pull a selection of beets. Slicing the Chioggia variety open reveals the perfect concentric red and white circles inside; they prefer the Bull's Blood variety that bleeds onto the ground when I cut it open. Some days, Jeanne-Marie takes them on her own farm tour, pointing out a secret bird's nest woven into the banana trees and other subtle signs of the farm's wildlife.

The smaller kids from the local elementary schools want to get their hands into everything except the worm box. I show them the paper and crop residues that have been thrown in and explain that it will be gone in a few days, consumed and turned into rich soil. I scoop up a handful of worms. Most of the kids back up slightly, a few come in for a closer look. No one touches.

121

From the Farmer's Son

At this time in America there are few kids growing up on farms, especially urban farms. Or at least I don't know of too many. I am one of those "few" and I felt it might be a good idea to write about my childhood growing up at Fairview Gardens.

I think the best thing is to talk about food. While peaches were my very first food and probably my favorite, there have also been cherimoyas, avocados, cucumbers, guavas, tomatoes, melons, mandarin oranges, and on and on. Each one of these foods didn't just have an effect on my body, but on my mind and on my soul as well. Most of my friends probably can't relate to the last part; they haven't had the experience of growing food, living with it, and tending it.

Most kids my age only know food from the shelf of a store; they don't understand the difficulties and joys of relying on your hands and the earth for a good meal each day. Although it may seem odd, I feel very close to the fresh food from the farm. I guess like anything else, when you are part of the process it grows on you. I think that kids who have a close connection to their food, who understand where it came from or took part in the process of growing or preparing it, have an easier time understanding other things as well.

Aaron Ableman

We pull a head of garlic and the kids close their eyes as I pass the fragrant bulb under each nose one by one. One "yuk" and they all chime in. I let them pick a strawberry. Just one, I say. "Look for the deep red, no green or white tips. Take your time. You only have one chance, so choose carefully." Some kids grab the first berry they see and inhale it; others move slowly examining dozens before picking the perfect one.

On a Friday evening in May, at my son's high school in Santa Ynez, California, we sat down to tiny machine-cut squares of carrots and turnips, mixed with corn and beans—succotash, I assume it said on the can. Outside within view of the dining hall is a ten-acre field bursting with red and green cabbages the size of basketballs, fifty cases worth of carrots, three beds of turnips, beets, artichokes, kale, chard, sweet onions, five types of lettuce, and enough strawberries to stuff each of the hundred students I'm sitting with until they cry uncle. The food in the fields has been slow to make it into the regular menus at the school.

The previous September, the students, their math teacher, some of the Fairview crew, and I faced a dry, dusty ten-acre pasture. We started by digging two-foot deep holes for fenceposts, and stretching wire for a three-quarter-mile fence to keep out the deer. Each day I'd bring a large watermelon from the farm to share at the end of the work session, and as a reminder of how our efforts and perseverance might eventually pay off.

I asked these kids to put their faith in the process that would take place in this empty field, to be patient and watch the unfolding events that would occur between planting and harvesting. I made an announcement at a school assembly. "Everyone who likes strawberries please raise your hands." Unanimous. "Well, there are a few steps between here and there, so I expect each of you who have your hand up (all of them) to be out in the garden helping." I added that by spring, if all went well, there would be enough strawberries for every student and teacher to gorge themselves sick. I could hear several students whisper to each other, "Yeah right."

Nine months later I was standing in the school garden trying to communicate with three students, who were sitting on the ground, their shirts and faces covered in red, and their stomachs bloated by strawberries. They could barely talk. The plants were dripping with unpicked fruit, the student body was tired of strawberries, and I was feeling quite smug.

Situated on three thousand acres surrounded by national forest, the farm here is as different from Fairview Gardens as it is possible to be. There are no highways, shopping centers, or housing developments, just a continuous uninterrupted view of mountains and open pasture. There are no sounds of traffic to interrupt the peace of the fields. However this is probably the only farm in North America where a person can hear a lion roar, an elephant trumpet, or a choo choo train whistle. The sounds

come from across Figueroa Mountain Road, where Michael Jackson's private amusement park Never Never Land is hidden from view.

When the first harvest of fresh vegetables was ready in the garden—radish, spinach, chard, kale, turnips, carrots, and lettuces—I offered to prepare a meal. I will never forget the students' pride and excitement over the first meal made exclusively from their garden. The kitchen director looked on, shaking his head at the obscenely large quantities of fresh vegetables heaped in bowls to be served to these high school students. "They'll never eat all that salad, nor the greens," he predicted.

The kids emptied every bowl. It wasn't hard to figure out why. They

125

Teaching Food and Farming to Children

Rather than explaining, provide the opportunity for experience. Create a point of focus immediately to gather children's energies together. Harvest something and eat it in the field together; wander around with no set agenda or particular rap. Be receptive to the kids and their observations and initiations. Speak from observation and feeling rather than intellect. Try not talking at all, just walk around a farm or garden silently listening, smelling, touching, and tasting. Remember that young people are bombarded with information. Context and interrelationships are valuable especially within a farm or garden. Most important, experience the joy of being together in nature.

had planted, hoed, and harvested the ingredients for this meal with their own hands. They watched the crops grow from seed, watered them, and protected them. This was not lettuce or broccoli or spinach arriving from who knows where.

Gardens are great teachers. Kids instinctively understand what they are learning when they grow things. The garden provides a learning environment where biology, botany, math, even physics come alive. The garden puts it all into context. It's not disconnected, free-floating information, but part of real life-problem solving. It's also easy to teach metaphors for life through the garden. Kids appreciate it when things make sense. They take it further than we expect, and see the big picture.

When I asked my sixteen-year-old son Aaron about this, I thought I knew what he'd say; we'd taught him the importance of fresh food. After all, he's the one who knows where to find the first ripe strawberry in a field of thousands of plants, or which tree in the orchards has the sweetest plums. He has always helped on the farm, sometimes enthusiastically, sometimes only with substantial persuasion. He'd been paying attention more than I really knew. Somehow this idea of a process, that food doesn't magically appear on store shelves, had taught him about the interconnection of other things.

Young people worry about crime, the ozone layer, war—a whole perilous world they perceive out there consuming their future. When they eat a meal they have grown and prepared they feel empowered. They have done something for themselves and for the planet. Aaron said part of what good food means to him is that some of the worries are set aside. It's something he can control.

My son tells me that kids at his age are thinking about their choices and developing their own minds. He suggests that it's more important to reach them than their parents. "You're not going to convince anyone by talking," my son cautioned me. "They've got to go out and try it, and see if they like it. They have to have an experience, that's what it really comes down to."

Without really planning to, all the people who worked on this land had built Fairview Gardens into a place where that experience could happen. National Public Radio and *National Geographic* came to comment on it and when the *Los Angeles Times* ran a front page article in 1997, we were inundated with calls and new visitors. I felt Fairview Gardens had found its mission.

At the same time, my employer Mrs. Chapman had been thinking about passing the land to her heirs. I had to face the fact that no matter how valuable it was to the community, this little farm was most valuable to the landowners as real estate. It seemed unlikely it would survive being handed down.

8.

The Next Hundred Years

Fairview Gardens grew into its present form under the shadow of zoning designation DR4.6: residential with the potential to develop fifty-eight houses. I lived and worked under this zoning. Feeling somewhat like a squatter and never quite sure of the future, I still planted and planned with the next generation in mind.

In 1993, the county scheduled a meeting to discuss removing the residential zoning from the land and redesignating it as agriculture. Considering that the property stands smack in the middle of a high density suburban neighborhood, this was an unusual move. Fairview's owner didn't tell me about this meeting; I found out about it the night before from a friend who works for the county.

When I walked into the planning commission hearing room, Cornelia's son asked what I was doing there. "You know what we plan to do with this land," he said, concerned that my public statement might influence the commission's decision. He had seen me in action before. A few minutes later, he had Cornelia on the nearby pay phone waiting to speak to me. In all the years I have known her, I have never heard her so angry. She said that if I spoke in favor of the down-zoning I would lose my job and be required to leave the farm. She emphasized that as a private property owner she had the right to provide for her heirs and that she didn't want to see the land become a "patch of weeds" sometime in the future.

I kept quiet that day, but the land was down-zoned anyway with the possibility for a reevaluation for development in ten years. For the moment the development pressure was off and the Chapman family could listen to ideas about a different kind of future for the land.

For seventeen years, Fairview Gardens has been my primary relationship. I have never known anything so deeply or so well. Few people have the chance to really *know* a piece of land, to watch it every day, year after year, and see, hear, smell, and feel its constant changes. Fairview makes it possi-

130

ble for other people to share this experience, to be nourished from the fields and orchards, and to learn and grow with the farm.

Fairview Gardens was never mine—and not just because someone else held the title. I have known for a long time that its role was to be a public place. It could never be just a private farm, or someone's personal retreat back to the land. Instead, this farm has provided a way for people to reclaim a connection to one of the most important and intimate acts: growing the food that they and their children eat. Over the course of a few generations, most people have given that power away to distant farms. They let this vital process take place out of sight, losing the pleasures and the connections that come with it.

We cannot all go back to the land, but we can provide something of the land to everyone. Fairview Gardens came to represent this opportunity, as do farmers' markets and community gardens throughout the world. The spotlight happened to fall on Fairview in part because of my own appetite for teaching, lecturing, and publicity. I quickly learned that high visibility was a tool to save this place and to bring attention to something that could be repeated elsewhere.

But the destiny of this farm was its own as well. The land exerted a powerful draw to the community, subtle at first, but finally so strong that many of our neighbors cannot now imagine giving up the farm. For me this is a small miracle. I have watched the developers sniff around the edges of this land and covet this last island for more houses. Yet parcel 69-90-52 has risen above anonymity to become a source of nourishment for so many.

I think that deep down Cornelia wanted Fairview to remain a farm, and to a great degree she was patient with the path I took here. Age, however, brought on the classic dilemma, and private property and public interests collided. Cornelia did not want to impose her will and values on her grown children though I believed with all my heart that she should. I believed that what she had to pass on was so much greater than real estate values and tax shelters. In a way, Fairview did not belong to Cornelia anymore either.

In 1994, I began to search for a way to give the Chapmans fair value for their land, while at the same time preserving it for the community. Some of the ideas interested Cornelia, and one day she left a small scrap of paper torn from a yellow legal pad on my kitchen counter. "Seven Hundred and Fifty Thousand Dollars Firm and No Bickering!" it said in her handwriting.

A small, committed group of local activists helped to form a nonprofit organization to buy the land and place it in a public trust. We agreed on Cornelia's price, but only after months of research and discussion to design the easement that would protect the land. This document is, in some ways, unlike anything that had been done before. Most conservation easements simply provide for open space. Our agreement with a local Land Trust specifies that the land must remain a working organic farm and that the educational work must continue under the nonprofit organization, officially named the Center for Urban Agriculture.

I could not believe what I had gotten myself into. Suddenly, after almost two decades of running the farm like a benevolent dictator, there was a board of directors, a 501 c3 nonprofit corporation, bylaws, a mission statement, and a fifty-page document that defined how the land could be used. By the time we were ready to sign the one-and-one-quarter-inch stack of legal papers and launch our fundraising effort, I had to wonder what all this had to do with tomatoes, healthy soil, and the life cycle of the oriental fruit moth.

In 1995, weeks before we were to celebrate the farm's one hundredth anniversary, I was out on the tractor discing the front field when I heard a clink. On an old tractor any noise can be expensive, so I quickly jumped off to assess the damage. There behind the blades of the disc was a perfectly preserved pestle. My friend, anthropologist John Johnson, said that it was used by the local Chumash Indians to grind acorns, possibly as long ago as two thousand years.

Soil is Everybody's Business

One of the results of our disconnection from the land has been the modern phenomena that we need "experts," "consultants," "farm advisors," and books like this one to tell us how to relate to the world of soil and plants. In traditional agrarian societies a child learned from riding on its mother's back while she worked in the fields or from apprenticeships. If you eat, soil is your business. Learn what good soil looks, feels, and smells like. Take a piece of land or a garden that has been abused and rebuild it; discover how to grow soil while growing food for yourself and your family. Believe in yourself. You are only two or three generations removed from the land.

My years on this land were suddenly put into perspective. Over centuries, my Chumash predecessors had left the land essentially unchanged. Now lawyers, appraisers, accountants, and endless luncheons, cocktail parties, and mailings were required to "save" the land.

Some people have asked why preserving this tiny farm is so important. There is farmland everywhere, they say. But this effort is not just about this little farm. Fairview Gardens is emblematic of what has happened all over this country. Small farms are disappearing at a staggering rate: forty-six acres of prime farmland are being converted to nonagricultural use each hour. I felt that if we could preserve this land in one of the most expensive real estate markets in the world, then our example could be used anywhere.

The farm is now 103 years old and after a monumental effort its future is secure. Knowing that it will always be a farm allows my mind to wander ahead to the next hundred years. I would like to see Fairview Gardens move beyond "organic" and explore what truly sustainable agriculture can be. We have made great strides here and succeeded in developing a local, low-impact food system, as well as a vital and ongoing relationship with the community. Now farm and community can explore the remaining challenges together.

For example, we are going to have to think more about water. My Hopi farmer friends and those farmers I met in parts of Africa and southern Europe know how to grow food with little water. They select crops that do not require sucking from deep aquifers and long distance pipelines. They also do not cool their foods using vast megawatts of electricity, nor do they use tractors that require constant fueling.

We can begin to question our practices even when the answers seem elusive. Everything we have done so far started with a question, and I believe that when we commit enough to ask, the answers always come.

Even at its best, farming is extractive. It consumes resources, both natural and human. Sustainable agriculture is often discussed in terms of the soils, air, and water. It rightfully addresses the distance food must travel and the impacts of farming on the environment. We must also look

at how well it sustains the people who do the work. It is a struggle to provide good wages, quality housing, health benefits, and a sense of ownership from a business that earns its annual budget by the pound.

Even so, Fairview Gardens employs twenty-one people and feeds close to five hundred families from twelve acres. It has proven to be a successful economic model, although never an easy one. The traditional bottom line does not consider the unpredictability of nature. It does not assign a value to soil fertility or the long term sustainability of land and community. I believe it should.

137

Some days, I feel a familiar stirring in my imagination. Maybe we could barter ears of corn or bunches of arugula for feed at the local feed store. We could pay our land taxes with boxes of carrots or sweet peppers, exchange fresh eggs and potatoes for tools and implements. Perhaps we should print our own "Fairview Dollars." I would replace the pictures of dead presidents with a portrait of a ladybug or perhaps a handful of soil with the motto, In God and *Land* We Trust.

I'm feeling a little less important around here these days. The crew knows the drill, our new organization is humming along, and all I want is to escape the telephone and get back out into the fields with a hoe in my hands. That is the kind of work that I came here to do. Now the farm has grown beyond me and my quiet revolution. Now it is time for me to let go. I can do so with the knowledge that whatever Fairview's future will bring, it will now be a collaboration and not just the big ideas of one crazy farmer.

When I first came to this farm, I worked alone. Quietly stumbling through the process of creating a farm, my hands were in the soil every day and all day. Over the years, we attracted young people wanting to learn, men from Mexico wanting to work, visitors from all over the world, and community members hungry for our fresh food. Now, after almost twenty years, Fairview Gardens has a life of its own.

Those who came forth and gave of their financial resources to secure this land are the final, crucial link in a chain that has been building for many years. But there would have been nothing to save were it not for all the people who have helped grow this farm and helped provide an anchor in a world that has been pulled from its roots in the earth.

Resources

TO CONTACT US

For more information about the programs at Fairview Gardens, to schedule a visit or farm tour, order any of our educational materials, or learn how to make a tax deductible contribution, please contact us at:

Center for Urban Agriculture
at Fairview Gardens
598 N. Fairview Avenue
Goleta, CA 93117
(805) 967-7369
Fax: (805) 967-0188
E-mail: FairviewG@aol.com
www. fairviewgardens. org

LAND CONSERVATION

Organizations
The American Farmland Trust
1920 North Street, NW
Washington, DC 20036
(202) 659-5170
Fax: (202) 659-8339

The Equity Trust
539 Beach Pond Road
Voluntown, CT 06384
Phone/Fax: (860) 376-6174

Institute for Community Economics
57 School Street
Springfield, MA 01105
(413) 746-8660

The Land Trust Alliance
1319 F Street NW, Suite 501
Washington, DC 20004
(202) 638-4725

The Trust for Public Land
33 Union Street, Fourth Floor
Boston, MA 02110-3306
(617) 367-6200

Publications
Community Land Trust Handbook.
Institute for Community Economics. Springfield, MA: Institute for Community Economics, 1982.
Avalable from Institute for Community Economics or The Equity Trust.

Doing Deals: A Guide to Buying Land for Conservation. Land Trust Alliance and The Trust for Public Land. Washington, DC: Land Trust Alliance and The Trust for Public Land, 1995.

Preserving Family Lands: Book Two. Stephen J. Small. Boston: The Landowner Planning Center, 1997.

Saving American Farmland: What Works. American Farmland Trust. Washington, DC: American Farmland Trust, 1997.

Holding our Ground: Protecting America's Farms and Farmland. Tom Daniels and Deborah Bowers. Washington, DC: Island Press, 1997.

COMMUNITY ACTION

Organizations
Community Alliance with Family Farmers
P.O. Box 363, Davis, CA 95617
(916) 756-8518; (800) 852-3832
Fax: (916) 756-7857
E-mail: caff@caff.org
Web site: www.caff.org

Institute for Trade and Agriculture Policy
2105 First Avenue South
Minneapolis, MN 55404
(612) 870-0453

140

Mothers and Others for a Livable Planet
40 West 20th Street, New York, NY 10011
(212) 242-0010 ext. 305
Fax: (212) 242-0545
E-mail: mothers@igc.apc.org

Pesticide Action Network North America
Regional Center
116 New Montgomery, Suite 810
San Francisco, CA 94105
(415) 541-9140; Fax: (415) 541-9253
E-mail: panna@panna.org
Web site: www.panna.org/panna

Public Voice for Food and Health Policy
1012 14th Street NW #800
Washington, DC 20005
(202) 347-6200
E-mail: hn2597@handsnet.org

Urban Agriculture Network
1711 Lamont Street NW
Washington, DC 20010
(202) 483-8130
E-mail: 72144.3446@compuserve.com

Publications
Basic Formula to Create Community Supported Agriculture. Robyn Van En. Great Barrington, MA: 1992.

Chicken Little, Tomato Sauce and Agriculture: Who Will Produce Tomorrow's Food? Joan D. Gussow. New York: The Bootstrap Press, 1991.

Community and the Politics of Place. Daniel Kemmis. Norman, OK: University of Oklahoma Press, 1991.

Community Related Agriculture: An Introduction. Bio-Dynamic Farming and Gardening Association. Kimberton, PA: Bio-Dynamic Farming and Gardening Association, Inc., 1994.

Community Supported Agriculture: An Annotated Bibliography and Resource Guide. S. Demuth. Beltsville, MD: National Agriculture Library, 1993.

Empty Breadbasket? The Coming Challenge to America's Food Supply and What We Can Do About It. The Cornucopia Project. Emmaus, PA: The Cornucopia Project, 1981.

For the Common Good: Redirecting the Economy Toward Community, the Environment, and a Sustainable Future. Herman Daly and John Cobb. Boston: Beacon Press, 1989.

From Land to Mouth: Understanding the Food System. Brewster Keen. Toronto, Canada: NC Press Limited, 1993.

The Good City and the Good Life. Daniel Kemmis. Boston: Houghton Mifflin, 1995.

Organizing a Local Cornucopia Project: A Manual for Changing Your Food System. The Cornucopia Project. Emmaus, PA: The Cornucopia Project, 1982.

Refashioning Nature: Food, Ecology and Culture. David Goodman and Michael Redclift. London: Routledge Press, 1991.

Sex, Economy, Freedom & Community. Wendell Berry. New York: Random House, Inc., 1992.

FOOD, AGRICULTURE & GARDENING

Organizations
American Community Gardening Association
100 Twentieth Street
N. Philadelphia, PA 19103
(215) 922-1508
E-mail: sallymmcc@libertynet.org

Bio-Dynamic Farming and Gardening
Association
P.O. Box 550, Kimberton, PA 19442
(800) 516-7797; Fax: (610) 983-3196

Canadian Organic Growers, Inc.
Box 6408, Station J
Ottawa, ON K2A 3Y6, Canada
(705) 444-0923; (613) 258-4045
Fax: (705) 444-0380
E-mail: organix@georgian.net;
eirving@cyberus.ca
Web site: www.gks.com/cog/

Center for Agroecology & Sustainable
Food Systems
1156 High Street
Santa Cruz, CA 95064
(408) 459-4140; Fax: (408) 459-2799

City Farmer
801 318 Homer Street
Vancouver, BC V6B 2V3, Canada
(604) 685-0431; Fax: (604) 685-0431
E-mail: cityfarm@unixg.ubc.ca

Committee for Sustainable Agriculture
406 Main Street #313
Watsonville, CA 95076
(408) 763-2111; Fax: (408) 763-2112

Community Alliance with Family Farmers
P.O. Box 363, Davis, CA 95617
(916) 756-8518; (800) 852-3832
Fax: (916) 756-7857
E-mail: caff@caff.org
Web site: www.caff.org

Ecological Agriculture Projects
21,111 Lakeshore Road
Ste. Anne de Bellevue
QC H9X 3V9, Canada
(514) 398-7771; Fax: (514) 398-7621
E-mail: eap@agradm.lan.mcgill.ca
Web site: www.agrenv.mcgill.ca/
extension/eap

Henry A. Wallace Institute for
Alternative Agriculture
9200 Edmonston Road, Suite 117
Greenbelt, MD 20770-1551
(310) 441-8777; Fax: (310) 220-0164

Land Stewardship Project
2200 4th Street
White Bear Lake, MN 55110
(612) 653-0618; Fax: (612) 653-0589

Leopold Center for Sustainable Agriculture
209 Curtiss Hall, Iowa State University
Ames, IA 50011-1050
(515) 294-3711; Fax: (515) 294-9696
E-mail: leocenter@iastate.edu

Mothers and Others for a Livable Planet
40 West 20th Street, New York, NY 10011
(212) 242-0010 ext. 305
Fax: (212) 242-0545
E-mail: mothers@igc.apc.org

Rodale Institute Experimental Farm
611 Siegfriedale Road
Kutztown, PA 19530
(610) 683-6383; Fax: (610) 683-8548
E-mail: info@rodaleinst.org

Seed Savers Exchange
3076 North Winn Road
Decorah, IA 52101
(319) 382-5990

Publications
*Backyard Market Gardening: The
Entrepreneur's Guide to Selling What You
Grow.* Andrew W. Lee. Burlington, VT:
Good Earth Publications, 1995.

*Common-Sense Pest Control: Least-Toxic
Solutions for Your Home, Garden, Pets &
Community.* Sheila Daar and William
Olkowski. New York: W.W. Norton & Co.,
1991.

Enduring Seeds—Native American Agriculture and Wild Plant Conservation. Gary Paul Nabham. Berkeley, CA: North Point Press, 1989.

Farms of Tomorrow—Community-Supported Farms, Farm-Supported Communities. Trauger Groh and Steven S. H. McFadden. Kimberton, PA: Bio-Dynamic Farming and Gardening Association, 1990.

From the Good Earth: A Celebration of Growing Food Around the World. Michael Ableman. New York: Harry Abrams, Inc., 1993.
Available from The Center for Urban Agriculture.

MetroFarm: The Guide to Growing for Big Profit on a Small Parcel of Land. Michael Oldon. Santa Cruz, CA: TS Books, 1994.

National Organic Directory. Community Alliance with Family Farmers. Davis, CA: Community Alliance with Family Farmers, 1997.

Our Sustainable Table. Edited by Robert Clark. San Francisco: North Point Press, 1990.

The Self-Sufficient Gardener. John Seymour. London: Faber & Faber, 1978.

Shattering—Food, Politics and the Loss of Genetic Diversity. Cary Fowler and Pat Mooney. Tucson, AZ: University of Arizona Press, 1990.

The Simple Act of Planting a Tree—Healing Your Neighborhood, Your City and Your World. Treepeople. Los Angeles: Jeremy P. Tarcher, 1990.

The Unsettling of America. Wendell Berry. San Francisco: Sierra Club Press, 1977.

EDUCATION

Organizations
The Common Roots Program
FoodWorks
64 Main Street
Montpelier, VT 05602
(802) 223-1515

Growing for Market
P.O. Box 3747
Lawrence, KS 66046
(800) 307-8949; Fax: (913) 841-2559

National Gardening Association
180 Flynn Avenue
Burlington, VT 05401
(802) 863-1308

Publications
Educational and Training Opportunities in Sustainable Agriculture. National Agricultural Library. Beltsville, MD: National Agricultural Library, 1994.

Toward a Sustainable Agriculture: A Teacher's Guide. The Sustainable Agriculture Curriculum Project. Madison, WI: University of Wisconsin Center for Integrated Agricultural Systems, 1991.

Acknowledgments

I want to thank the many people who have generously contributed their work and energy to building and preserving the farm, in particular: Chris Thompson who provided me with a foundation to build on; Salvador Gomez for his many years of keeping things going in the fields during my absences; the late Roger Chapman who shared my vision for the farm; Cornelia Chapman for her ongoing support; Jean Schuyler for her tireless fundraising efforts; Donna my friend and ex-wife for her hard work during the beginning years on the land; my dear son, Aaron, whose presence has kept me in one place all these years; and to Jeanne-Marie for her love, loyalty, and friendship.

For the book I wish to thank Cynthia Wisehart, without whom this book could not have happened. To Sandy Lejuene, Abe Lieder, Thomas Cole, Aurreliano Avina, and the rest of the farm crew who held things together during this process, and to the Becks, the Esalen Institute, and the Midland School for providing me quiet places to write. I would like to thank my agent Martha Casselman, Laura Lovett for her design, and Leslie Jonath for her commitment to this project and her persistance in seeing it through.